Alitalia

From Glory to Collapse

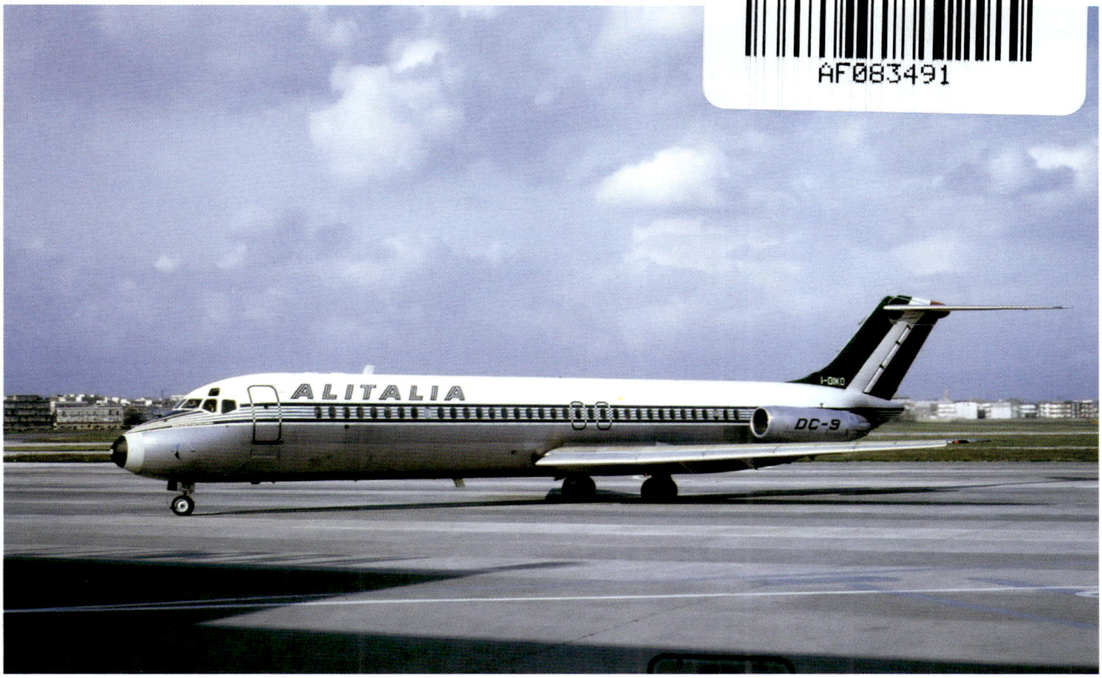

JOZEF MOLS

KEY Books

AIRLINES SERIES, VOLUME 16

Front cover image: An Alitalia Douglas MD-82. (Thijs Postma)

Title page image: A Douglas DC-9. (Jozef Mols)

Contents page image: An Avro RJ70 from Alitalia's franchise partner Azzurra Air. (Jozef Mols)

Back cover image: One of the last Airbus A320s to be delivered to Alitalia. (Alitalia)

Published by Key Books
An imprint of Key Publishing Ltd
PO Box 100
Stamford
Lincs PE9 1XQ

www.keypublishing.com

The right of Jozef Mols to be identified as the author of this book has been asserted in accordance with the Copyright, Designs and Patents Act 1988 Sections 77 and 78.

Copyright © Jozef Mols, 2023

ISBN 978 1 80282 676 0

All rights reserved. Reproduction in whole or in part in any form whatsoever or by any means is strictly prohibited without the prior permission of the Publisher.

Typeset by SJmagic DESIGN SERVICES, India.

Contents

Introduction and Acknowledgements 4
Chapter 1   The Origins 6
Chapter 2   Nationalism 9
Chapter 3   A New Start 18
Chapter 4   The Merger 31
Chapter 5   Troubles Ahead 41
Chapter 6   The 1990s 48
Chapter 7   Crisis 56
Chapter 8   CAI-Alitalia 60
Chapter 9   New Crisis 62
Chapter 10   Etihad 70
Chapter 11   Hope in Vain 72
Chapter 12   Government Control 74
Chapter 13   New Bidders 77
Chapter 14   Epilogue: ITA Airways 80
Appendix 1   Incidents and Accidents 83
Appendix 2   Fleet Details 87
Appendix 3   Notes and References 90

Introduction and Acknowledgements

Italy's aviation industry emerged, as in many other European countries, during World War One when attempts were made to design and build entire aircraft. Some of these aircraft would become famous after they participated in international competitions such as the Schneider Trophy, and in 1925, Francesco de Pinedo made the first long-distance flight from Brindisi to Australia; yet Italy was one of the last countries in Europe to set up civil aviation services. The Alps and Apennines prevented regular civil air travel within Italy for a long time. Eventually, several smaller airlines took to the sky, and the 1930s were a time of consolidation that saw the merger of many of these companies. Ala Littoria, the result of this merger, gave Benito Mussolini's government an opportunity to showcase the country's resources and increase its influence in countries across the Mediterranean and Africa, but when Italy joined Nazi Germany in World War Two, civilian aircraft were taken over by the Servizi Aerei Speciali (Special Air Services) to transport Italian troops and supplies.

Once World War Two was over, there was a burst of civil aviation activity. Many airlines were set up or re-emerged after being grounded during the war, and some of the new airlines started up with foreign assistance, such as Aerolinea Italiane Internazionale S.p.A. This company used the brand name Alitalia and was established in 1946 with the participation of British European Airways (BEA). In 1957, the Istituto per la Ricostruzione Industriale (IRI, Institute for Industrial Reconstruction) – which controlled both Alitalia and the main competing airline, Linee Aeree Italiana (LAI) – decided to merge the two airlines under the Alitalia brand name, thus consolidating the Italian transport market.

The 1960 Summer Olympic Games in Rome were a milestone for Alitalia, which became the official carrier. The airline introduced its first jets, including the French Caravelle and the American Douglas DC-8. New social benefits, such as paid holidays for workers, resulted in an increased demand for air transportation, and as Italy became a favourite holiday spot for many Europeans, Alitalia benefited from this evolution and had to order larger jets such as the Boeing 747. But inflation and political instability in Italy would soon cause problems for its flag carrier, and large debts, persistent losses and falling revenues were the result. During the 1980s, Alitalia went through a substantial restructuring and the airline became profitable again in 1987. But it was not yet out of troubled waters. Disruptive strikes by pilots, cabin staff and ground crew were the result of general weakness in the long-term planning by the management. Soon, it became clear the airline would only be able to survive within an international alliance. Talks were started with KLM Royal Dutch Airlines, but the cooperation project would not materialise. At the turn of the millennium, Alitalia's downward spiral started in earnest. European deregulation of minimum fare pricing created tight competition across the continent. The Italian government had to pump money into the airline to support it following labour disputes, and politicians and 'political influencers' entered the boardrooms of the airline. When Alitalia's survival was at stake, Silvio Berlusconi's government gave several loans to the airline, rather than accepting propositions by other European carriers to buy shares in the ailing flag carrier, and although Alitalia was having to fight to survive, its management decided in this crucial period to take over other ailing Italian airlines. In 2007, Alitalia was on the brink of collapse, and the airline accepted the offer from Air France-KLM to participate in its capital through an injection of fresh money. But Berlusconi railed against the deal just before the political elections in Italy. In 2008, Alitalia went bankrupt for the first time.

Immediately, a new carrier was set up as CAI-Alitalia, which took over the 'healthy parts' of Alitalia. But soon the 'new' carrier was also in trouble. The Italian government tried to facilitate a takeover of Alitalia by Etihad Airways, resulting in a joint venture between Alitalia and Etihad. For the Arab carrier, however, it soon became clear political meddling and nepotism would continue to cause problems. In 2017, Etihad refused to further inject cash into the joint venture and Alitalia went bankrupt for a second time. The Italian government had no choice but to take over the airline while trying to sell it to potential bidders. Several carriers expressed their interest in taking over Alitalia, either as a whole or by taking a share in the capital. Finally, in 2023, Lufthansa obtained a 41 per cent participation in the newly established and government-controlled carrier, which now operates under the brand name Italia Trasporto Aereo (ITA). In the meantime, the Italian taxpayer had lost over €8bn (£6.89bn) over the previous seven years due to government subsidies and loans to keep Alitalia in the air.

I was only able to write the story of Alitalia with the help of aviation historians, libraries, research institutions, specialised journalists and the many photographers who provided the pictures that illustrate this book. Special thanks go to my partner, Marianne Van Leuvenhaege, who encouraged me during researching the subject and writing the book and who was my first proofreader. Of course, my gratitude also goes to Key for publishing and distributing this book.

Jozef Mols,
Wommelgem (Belgium)
10 June 2023

Alitalia was chosen to transport several popes on their trips. Here we see Pope Benedict XVI arriving at the 316th Wing at Andrews Air Force Base, Washington, D.C. (U.S. Air Force photo by Tech. Sgt. Suzanne M. Day, Public domain, via Wikimedia Commons)

Chapter 1
The Origins

While Italy may have gone on to become a major European player when it came to aircraft design and construction, at the beginning of World War One, the country was not yet able to design or build an entire aircraft, even though it produced engines. But wars drive countries to invest as much as possible in research and production, and this was also the case in Italy. In 1916, the country started to seriously engage in the aeronautical industry, resulting in models such as the Ansaldo SVA being built. One of these aircraft flew over Vienna in 1918 to pitch thousands of flyers, inviting the Austrians to surrender. It was also during the war that the first Italian aviation pioneers wrote their names in history books. Mario de Bernardi was a fighter pilot who obtained his pilot's licence in 1914. He would become the first Italian credited with destroying an enemy aircraft in the air. By the end of the war, de Bernardi had received credit for the destruction of four Austro-Hungarian aircraft. After the war, he started racing seaplanes in international races, which were very popular at that time. His greatest success came on 13 November 1926, when he won the Schneider Trophy race at Hampton Roads, Virginia, US, flying a Macchi M.39. On 30 March 1928, he would become the first person to exceed the speed of 310mph (500km/h), when he flew a Macchi M.52R racing seaplane, and he would go on to become test pilot for the Caproni company in Taliedo near Milan.[1]

Francesco de Pinedo would enter the scene a little later, having first served in the Regia Marina (Royal Italian Navy) before obtaining his pilot's licence in 1918. During the last months of World War One, he would fly reconnaissance missions for the navy. In the immediate post-war years, he would make milestone flights from Italy to the Netherlands, and in 1921 from Brindisi to Constantinople (now Istanbul) in the Ottoman Empire. In 1923, he transferred from the Regia Marina to the Regia Auronautica (Royal Italian Air Force), which had been founded that year. Just like de Bernardi, he firmly believed in the potential of seaplanes. On 21 April 1925, Pinedo and his mechanic, Ernesto Campanelli, departed Rome aboard a SIAI S-16ter flying boat, which he named *Gennariello*. A first stop was made in Rome, after which he flew via Brindisi to Leros in Greece, Baghdad in Iraq, Busher and Chabar in Persia, Karachi, Bombay, and Calcutta in British India, Rangoon in Burma, Phuket in Siam, Penang and Singapore, Batavia, Surabaya, Sumbawa and Kupang in the Netherlands East Indies, and finally Broome, Carnarvon, Perth, Bunbury, Albany, Israelite Bay, Adelaide and Melbourne in Australia. After a three-week stop in Sydney, he continued his trip via the Netherlands East Indies and the Philippines to Shanghai in China, Mokpo in Korea and Yamakawa and Kagoshima in Japan, before arriving in Tokyo on 26 September. The return journey to Rome took 22 days.[2]

Mussolini suggested that Pinedo also make a flight to the Western hemisphere to inspire pride in people of Italian ancestry who had migrated to the Americas. This idea would develop into the 'Four Continents' flight in 1927, during which de Pinedo flew from Italy via the Cape Verde Islands to Brazil. After stops at various cities in South America, the Italians flew over the dense jungle of Brazil's Mato Grosso. Along their trip, they also visited the Caribbean and arrived in New Orleans on 29 March 1927. This was the first time a foreign aircraft had flown into the United States.[3]

Regia Aeronautica General Italo Balbo relied heavily on Pinedo's advice when planning and executing the mass formation flights intended to improve aircrews' operational skills, but above all to showcase the Italian aviation industry and enhance the prestige of Mussolini's Italian Fascist government. Balbo himself would lead the first of these mass flights, in which 51 Savoia-Marchetti S-59bis and ten Savoia-Marchetti S55s were involved. In 1930, Balbo would lead another transatlantic flight of 12 Savoia-Marchetti S.55 flying boats from Orbetello seaplane base in Italy to Rio de Janeiro. In July 1933, 24 Italian seaplanes would fly roundtrip from Rome to the Century of Progress in Chicago, Illinois.[4]

Although Italy amassed considerable experience in military and naval aviation before 1920, the country would be one of the last in Europe to begin civil aviation services. It had its fingers in military projects but took longer to take the leap in the civil sector. Political instability may have been one of the contributing factors, but geography also played a part in Italy's late start, since the Alps and the Apennines prevented regular civil air travel within Italy. Not until the mid-1920s, a good five years after the rest of the major European powers, did Italy become a major participant in European commercial aviation.[5] As happened in most other European countries, several small companies initially formed that struggled to provide a modest level of passenger service. In Lusinpiccolo, at that time located on the island of Lussino, which was Italian territory (today, it is part of Croatia), the Società Italiana Servizi Aerei SISA SpA was founded by the brothers Callisto and Alberto Cosulech. They were both shareholders of the Trieste Naval Shipyard. In 1924, SISA started up flights between Venice and Trieste. Later on, a Trieste–Turin–Trieste route was added. In its early days, SISA had a fleet of four CANT 10 seaplanes, which could transport five passengers each. Additionally, the company also had a CANT 7 for training purposes, which was later also used on scheduled services. In 1926, the network was expanded to include flights from Trieste and Pula to Ancona and Zadar. Later on, a Brindisi–Vlora (Albania) service was also inaugurated.

The first modern aviation operation, founded by the government, was Aero Expresso Italiana (AEI). Formed on 12 December 1923, it would take three more years for the first AEI flight to take off. On 19 January 1925, Società Anonima Navigazione Aerea (SANA) was formed by the Banca Comerciale Italiana with a stock capital of a million Lire (L), divided over 10,000 shares of L100 each. The official aim of the company was to open national and international air routes to be operated by seaplanes. In April 1925, the airline received concessions for the operation of the Genova–Barcelona and Genova–Brindisi air routes. The concession was valid for ten years and the company could count on a subsidy for flights of up to 640,000km (397,677 miles) per year. On 7 April 1926, the Genoa–Rome–Naples–Palermo route was opened using seaplanes built in Marina di Pisa under licence from Dornier. In 1929, collaboration started with Imperial Airways on the Italy to Egypt route, associated with the British flight to India. A flight from Syracuse to Tripoli was also inaugurated.[6]

In 1925, the Società Anonima Di Navigazione Aerea Transadriatica (Transadriatica) was set up by Renato Morandi and his brother Mario in cooperation with Domenico Giuriati, a former military pilot. The airline was supported by Junkers GmbH. During the first months of its existence, the airline operated flights from the seaplane base in Ancona, using Macchi M.18 aircraft. However, on 18 April 1926, it was decided to move the operation to Venice. Soon a Venice–Rome route was started up. Later on, an international service was inaugurated from Venice via Klagenfurt to Vienna in cooperation with the Austrian airline OLAG, using a Junkers F.13 (I-BATB) aircraft. A further five aircraft of the same type (I-BATC, I-BAVB, I-BBAS, I-BBCA and I-AEDO) entered the fleet soon after. Starting in 1927, two Junkers G.24s (I-BAUS and I-BAZI) replaced the smaller F13s on the Venice–Vienna route. In 1928, a route from Brindisi to Munich was opened. In 1931, the route from Rome to Munich was opened in cooperation with Lufthansa.[7] In the meantime, a Junkers W.34 (I-AAMA) and a Hamilton 47 (I-ROMA) had joined the fleet.

Società Aerea Mediterranea (SAM), on the other hand, operated cargo and passenger routes from its base in Rome. The airline had been founded as a government initiative of Italo Balbo, by then the

Secretary of State for Air. The airline used a fleet of Caproni and Savoia-Marchetti flying boats.[8] In December 1931, SAM merged with Transadriatica.[9]

By 1930, the three biggest airlines (SISA, SANA, and SAM) equally split the Italian civil aviation market, carrying about 10,000 passengers per year. If, in 1925, it seemed as if the Italians hardly had a civil aviation sector, by 1930 they had made rapid progress. The Italian commercial aviation sector had become the third largest in Europe in terms of the number of passengers carried, after Germany and France, and ahead of Great Britain and the Netherlands. Most Italian routes were limited to locations geographically close to the country, such as Germany, the Italian territories in North Africa (particularly Libya), Greece, Turkey, France, and Austria. The 1930s were a time of consolidation for the European aviation sector, and Italy was no exception. In August 1934, SAM, SANA and SISA were merged to form a single national airline known as Ala Littoria, which was owned by the government.[10] The new state-owned outfit gave Mussolini's government an opportunity to showcase the country's resources and to increase its influence in other countries across the Mediterranean and Africa.[11]

One airline, however, would remain independent: Avio Linee Italiane (ALI). The airline was owned by the Fiat Group and would operate between 1926 and 1952. It started passenger services between Rome and Munich in May 1928 and extended the route to Berlin in 1931. The airline operated a fleet of seven Fokker F.VII aircraft. During the 1930s, the airline expanded its service to include other Italian cities and, beginning in 1938, it added the Venice–Milan–Turin–Paris–London route.[12]

Italo Balbo, the father of Italian civil aviation. (Unknown author, public domain, attraverso Wikimedia Commons, www.audiovis.nac.gov.pl)

Chapter 2
Nationalism

Civilian aircraft used during the first years of regular air transportation were mainly made in Germany (Dornier Wal and Super Wal, Junkers G.24 and F.13) and the Netherlands (Fokker F.VIIB). But when nationalism rose in the 1940's, aircraft produced in Italy became more fashionable.[1] These were mostly bombers converted for civilian use, such as the three-engine Savoia-Marchetti S.73.[2] Unsurprisingly, Rome was the main Italian airport, but Venice would remain the second base of the Ala Littoria. Most of the maintenance of its aircraft also took place in Venice,[3] by technicians trained during the period of cooperation between Transadriatica and Junkers. The airline managed to start up flights to many European destinations. But above all, Ala Littoria played an important role in controlling Italy's colonial empire in North and East Africa. In establishing routes from Italy to Africa, the airline had to overcome many geographic obstacles. For example, airplanes of the 1930s had great difficulty reaching Asmara, the capital of Eritrea, a part of Italian East Africa, which is located about 4,547m (15,000ft) above sea level.[4]

SANA had actually been the first Italian airline to fly to Africa when it started a Rome–Tripoli route in 1928, using a Dornier Superwal, and later on the Geneva–Alessandria route.[5] In 1934, an experimental flight from Rome to Mogadishu in Somalia was organised by Ala Littoria. The initiative came as a result of the visit by King Vittorio Emanuele III to Italy's African colonies. For this occasion, the Italian Post Office issued special stamps only valid for airmail on this flight. Francis Lombardi took off from Rome with his Savoia-Marchetti S.71 and made refuelling stops in Tobruk and Massawa (Eritrea).[6] The flight would establish a world record for long-distance civil flights and would later allow the start of the prestigious Linea dell'Impero (Imperial Line),[7] which would become the longest route in Africa by Ala Littoria and was considered the most prestigious Italian air route. In the beginning, however, the line would be operated in cooperation with Britains Imperial Airways, which transported passengers from Rome via Brindisi and Cairo to Khartoum. In Khartoum, an Ala Littoria aircraft would await the passengers to bring them to Asmara and further to Massawa, Djibouti and Galadi (Somalia) to Mogadishu. Later on, the flight was rerouted, and passengers would leave from Rome via Syracuse to Benghazi. In the Libyan city, they would spend the night at the Berenice Hotel before continuing their trip by Savoia-Marchetti S.73 (and later Savoia-Marchetti S.75). This final portion would take them from Benghazi via Cairo, Khartoum, Cassala (Sudan), Asmara and Addis Ababa to Mogadishu.[8]

In the meantime, Ala Littoria had stipulated, in a 1935 agreement with the Albanian government, that it would take over and manage the lines of the Albanian network. By that time, Ala Littoria had added a single Savoia-Marchetti SM-84 to its fleet, as well as nine Savoia S.66 flying boats. These aircraft had twin hulls, and each hull could seat up to seven passengers, while the pilot was seated in the wing centre section. On 7 May 1935, Ala Littoria also entered into agreements with KLM and Deutsche Luft Hansa, inaugurating the Milan–Frankfurt–Amsterdam route. A similar agreement with Air France made it possible to start up a daily Rome–Marseilles–Paris route, using Savoia S.74 and Potez 62 aircraft. The S.74 was, because of its large dimensions, almost a 'jumbo' at that time with a luxurious cabin for 24 passengers, and it was equipped with a bar and toilet. Only three such aircraft were ever built. In 1936, Ala Littoria signed an agreement with the Greek government in order to start up the Rome–Brindisi–Athens–Rhodes and Brindisi–Tirana–Thessaloniki routes. On 7 April 1937, an important route between Italy and Palestine was inaugurated. Starting in 1939, this route would be extended to Baghdad and Basra.[9] By 1938, Ala Littoria had become the most important carrier in Africa, even ahead of Air France. It is clear the airline had become a major tool in the construction of the Italian empire.[10] In Europe, new capitals were reached with the Venice–Klagenfurt–Bratislava–Prague route and the Rome–Belgrade–Bucharest line. Also, services to warring Spain were secured, including the Rome–Pollensa–Cadiz line. Starting from 25 April 1938, passengers were also able to fly from Lisbon to Rome via Seville–Malaga–Melilla and Palma de Mallorca.[11]

Once the national, colonial and European networks were organised, Ala Littoria began to focus its attention beyond the Atlantic. On 20 March 1938, the first experiment of a regular connection between Italy and Latin America took place on the Rome–Cagliari–Bathurst (now Banjul in Gambia)–Bahia–Rio de Janeiro–Buenos Aires route. The CANT Z 506 seaplane was flown by Carlo Tonini and the president of the airline itself, Umberto Klinger. This route would later be operated by Linee Aeree Transcontinentale Italiane (LATI). It would operate the services between 1939 and 1941, when the United States entered the war.

The total network reached its maximum development in 1939, reaching 23,059 miles (37,110km) with a fleet of 101 aircraft of various types. Nevertheless, the airline remained one of the smallest major airlines in Europe in terms of market capitalisation and route network size, when compared to KLM, Deutsche Luft Hansa and Imperial Airways.[12] It remained dependent on government subsidies in order to remain commercially viable. Its existence was largely dependent on its political value, as an unprofitable failing national airline would have been an unwelcome sign of failure of the Italian regime.[13] But such a situation was not an anomaly in the 1930s. In the US, airlines also depended on government contracts, and losses by KLM during the interwar period were absorbed by government subsidies. In 1937, Ala Littoria reported that 87,342 passengers had flown on its routes in the previous year. This represented about 76 per cent of all passenger traffic on Italian airlines, confirming Ala Littoria's dominant position. Expansion plans included a connection between Rome and Tokyo, but this plan depended on the commissioning of suitable four-engined aircraft types. Connections to the US were also planned to start in 1942.[14]

However, Ala Littoria's expansion plans were halted by the onset of World War Two. The great majority of Italy's civil air fleet was mobilised for military duties in 1940. Airlines were placed under an umbrella organisation known as the Comando Servizi Aerei Speciali or Special Air Services Wing. Ala Littoria could only continue to operate connections between Italy and Germany, using Junkers Ju-52 aircraft.[15] It would not survive the war. Avio Trasporti was incorporated in 1938 to operate routes within the Italian colonies in Africa using Caproni CA 148 aircraft. These included a line between Rome and Assab, although this never actually started. But just like Ala Littoria, it did not survive the war. The CANT Z 506 seaplanes of LATI were also taken over by the military.

The only airline to escape incorporation into Ala Littoria was ALI, owned by Fiat. ALI started passenger services between Rome and Munich in May 1928 and extended the service to Berlin in 1931. The company further expanded its network to other Italian cities and also operated at least one international route, Venice–Milan–Turin–Paris–London. In 1935, the carrier obtained several Savoia-Marchetti SM 73 aircraft. On the first flight to Asmara, the aircraft carried some 200,000 letters. In the following months, the aircraft would be used on routes connecting Rome with Berlin and Rome with different destinations in Greece. In 1938, the Savoia-Marchetti SMx.75 joined the fleet. This long-range aircraft was used on routes to Tokyo and to the United States (until the US joined the war in Europe). As of 1939, ALI had a fleet of 16 aircraft, including one DC-2 (I-EROS), nine Fiat G.18/G.18V and six Savoia-Marchetti aircraft. In 1940, a few Macchi MC 100 aircraft were added, to be used on the Rome–Alghero–Barcelona route. When Italy joined Nazi Germany in World War Two, these aircraft would be used to transport Italian troops and supplies to North Africa. Soon, however, the entire fleet would also be taken over by the Servizi Aerei Speciali. During the war, at least one S.73 and four G.18s were lost in operational accidents during the war.[16]

An old postcard, depicting an Ala Littoria Savoia-Marchetti S.74. (Scanne par Claude Shoshany, Public domain, attraverso Wikimedia Commons)

The Savoia-Marchetti S.74 was used on many Ala Littoria routes. (Thijs Postma collection)

A Savoia-Marchetti S.74 ready for departure. (Thijs Postma collection)

The cabin of Ala Littoria's Savoia-Marchetti S.74. (Thijs Postma collection)

Above: In 1934, this letter was sent by airmail to Mogadishi aboard an Ala Littoria aircraft.
(Public domain, Jozef Mols collection)

Right: An Ala Littoria vintage poster, promoting the routes to Italy's African colonies.
(Ala Littoria, public domain, Jozef Mols collection)

Ala Littoria used a CANT Z 506 to prepare its regular services to Latin America. (Thijs Postma)

An Ala Littoria SM.79, used on the route to Brazil. (Public domain, Wikimedia Commons)

Ala Littoria also obtained nine S.66 flying boats. (Thijs Postma collection)

An Ala Littoria Savoia-Marchetti SM.84 in Switzerland. (Unknown author, public domain, via Wikimedia Commons)

The Savoia-Marchetti SM.84 was used on both European and North African routes. (Unknown author, public domain, via Wikimedia Commons)

In 1935, Ala Littoria obtained the Savoia-Marchetti SM.73. (Thijs Postma collection)

Above: An Ala Littoria Savoia-Marchetti SM.75 long range aircraft. (Thijs Postma collection)

Left: The Macchi M.C.100 entered service in 1940. (Thijs Postma collection)

Shortly before the war, the M.C.100 was used on routes linking Rome with Alghero and Barcelona. (Thijs Postma collection)

During World War Two, the M.C.100 was used to transport troops and equipment to North Africa. (Thijs Postma collection)

Chapter 3
A New Start

When Italy resumed commercial aviation operations in the post-war era, there was a burst of activity.[1] Airlines that had been absorbed during the nationalisation campaign in 1934 got permission to start up activities again as independent carriers. The Cosulich family took the initiative and SISA once again appeared on the scene. The airline bought seven surplus military Douglas C-47s from the US Air Force, and these aircraft were converted to civil transport in Venice. Once this was done, the airline started up its flights from the 'Amedeo Duca d'Aosta' airport in Gorizia. Soon agreements were made with the Czechoslovak, Yugoslav, Greek and Turkish aviation authorities to establish reciprocal air links between the capitals. SISA would continue its activities until May 1949.

After two years of preparation, another airline, Airone, began operating from the airfield of Monserrato on 15 April 1947. Airone used Fiat G-12 aircraft. Because of high costs, the aircraft's Fiat A.74 R.C.42 14-cylinder air-cooled radial piston engines were soon replaced by Pratt & Whitney engines. However, even with these changes, the airline could only run because it initially held a state-granted monopoly on routes to Rome, and its aircraft would be used on routes connecting Sardinia with Rome and Milan. The airline continued to operate until the end of 1949.[2]

Transadriatica from Venice would operate the first post-war flight between Venice and Rome on 14 April 1947. The airline was incorporated by Leonida Schiona, a former Regia Aeronautica pilot. The fleet consisted of converted Douglas C-47B aircraft on loan from the Italian government. In December 1947, Transadriatica inaugurated its first international service from Venice to Zürich Dübendorf.

ALI was also reconstituted, and in 1947, the airline ordered six Fiat G.212's from its parent company, Fiat. At some point, it also acquired at least one C-47. In 1949, ALI would merge with Airone (also a Fiat operator) and Transadriatica to form ALI-Flotti Riunite (ALI Reunited Fleets). The combined fleet consisted of seven Fiat G.12s and a dozen C-47s. Its timetable showed routes to Barcelona, Paris, Brussels, Amsterdam, Frankfurt, Prague, Vienna and Athens. The airline would continue its operations until 1952.[3]

The Italians were not the only ones to invest in new airlines following World War Two. Britain and the United States had been allies with Italy since 1947, and Transcontinental & Western Air (TWA) and BEA played a major role in the creation of Italian carriers. They contributed to the restoration of Italian commercial aviation by financing the establishment of two major Italian airlines: Aerolinee Italiane Internazionale (operating under the brand name Alitalia) and LAI. These airlines would serve as the backbone of Italian civil air activity into the 1950s, together with ALI-Flotti Riunite.[4]

On 16 September 1946, LAI was incorporated. TWA had 40 per cent of the shares, while the IRI obtained a 60 per cent share. The American participation would soon be contested within the Italian government as Italian law prescribed that Italian investors should at least own two thirds of the shares of any airline set up in the country. Therefore, Fiat (7 per cent), Italian railways company Società Italiana per le Strade Ferrate Meridionali (7 per cent) and Italian motorbike manufacturer Piaggio (6 per cent) also became shareholders in early 1947, thus increasing the Italian share of the capital to the legal requirements. In April 1947, the airline inaugurated its first flights from the Rome Urbe airport to a series of Italian destinations. The fleet consisted of war surplus American Douglas DC-3 aircraft. In the same year, LAI started up international services to Athens, Istanbul and Tunis. Most of the pilots were former military pilots from the Regia Auronautica.[5] In 1950, the airline obtained four Douglas DC-6 aircraft, which not only had a larger capacity than the DC-3s, but also offered more passenger comfort.[6] By 1952, competitor ALI-Flotte Riunite had been liquidated and the carrier was subsequently acquired by LAI. In 1954, another four Douglas DC-6Bs joined the airline. By that time, LAI had become the most important airline in Italy. It is certain LAI could only have grown this way thanks to the support from its American shareholder, which had made its experience and know-how available, as well as its money. With the DC-6, the airline was also able to start up the prestigious Rome–Paris–New York route. The airline had become the first Italian post-war carrier to operate the transatlantic route. In 1953, the airline had also added four Convair CV-240s to its fleet to be used on domestic and regional routes. In the same year, LAI operated 25 domestic routes alongside 22 international and 12 intercontinental services and its aircraft had flown 7.6 million km (5.722 million miles) and transported 151,000 passengers.[7] In order to finance the expansion of the airline, LAI had obtained a $4.5m loan from the Economic Cooperation Administration, which made it possible to buy aircraft in the US.[8] Unfortunately, on 24 November 1956, one of LAI's DC-6B's (I-LEAD) en route from Paris to New York crashed soon after take-off, killing 34 of the 35 people on board. By the end of the year, however, LAI ordered four Lockheed L-1649 Starliners to be used on the transatlantic route. All aircraft had already been built and painted in LAI colours when the order was cancelled, as LAI merged with Aerolinea Italiane Internazionale. Just before this merger, LAI had also obtained a number of Vickers Viscount aircraft.

While the American airline TWA was investing in the Italian civil aviation sector by helping to establish LAI, BEA was also active by taking a participation in Aerolinea Italiane Internazionale, which used the brand name 'Alitalia'. The airline was established in September 1946. The initial British investment amounted to an initial L900m and an additional investment of L1.5bn by the start of 1947. The company began operations in the spring of that year with two three-engined Fiat G.12s, flying the Turin–Rome and Rome–Catania routes.[9] Still the same year, the first international route from Rome to Oslo was inaugurated. The 38 passengers flying on this route flew in a Savoia-Marchetti SM.95. The airline had obtained four such aircraft, but as these models were not pressurised passengers and crew were required to wear oxygen masks on flights over the Alps. Both the Fiat's and Savoia-Marchetti's were obtained on loan from the Regia Auronautica. By the end of the year, the airline had transported 10,306 passengers and 110 tons of cargo over a network that covered 9,000km (5,592 miles). The staff of the airline consisted of 300 people, of which 55 where flight crew.[10]

In March 1948, the airline acquired several four-engined Avro Lancastrian 691 MK3 aircraft, derived from the Avro Lancaster bomber.[11] That year, Alitalia would inaugurate its first intercontinental service, introducing flights from Rome to Buenos Aires via Dakar, Natal and Rio de Janeiro. The flight would last about 30 hours. In 1950, Alitalia CEO Niccolo Carrandini, who had replaced the first chairman Guiseppe de Micheli in 1948, decided to replace the entire fleet with one Douglas DC-3 and four DC-4s. Alitalia's resolve was rewarded in 1952 with its first profitable year. By 1955, the airline once again replaced its entire fleet, this time acquiring four Convair 340s for short- to medium-haul routes and four DC-6Bs for long-range routes.[12] In this period, the first flight attendants were introduced with uniforms designed by the fashion house Sorelle Fontana.[13] Hot meals were served with a high-quality and refined selection of food and beverages. Expansion continued throughout the 1950s. By the tenth anniversary of the airline in 1956, its aircraft had travelled a total of 48,630km (30,000 miles) and had transported a total of 116,394 passengers. The number of employees had risen to 1,120 and the company's capital to L4.5bn.[14] What is most important, however, was that the airline had earned enough profit to cover the losses remaining from its early years.[15]

Airone used a fleet of Fiat G.12 aircraft. (Thijs Postma collection)

An Airone timetable from 1949. (Björn Larsson collection, via www.timetableimages.com)

This 1949 timetable of Airone shows the different destinations served by the airline. (Björn Larsson collection, via www.timetableimages.com)

A Transadriatica delegation arrives in Zürich to negotiate landing rights. (ETH-Bibliothek Zürich, public domain)

A Transadriatica Douglas DC 3 in Zürich in 1947. (ETH-Bibliothek Zürich, public domain)

A Fiat G.212 of Avio Linee Italiane (ALI). (Thijs Postma collection)

Above: An ALI Fiat G.212 is being prepared for another flight from the Zürich airport. (http://ba.e-pics.ethz.ch/#1461776195066_9, CC BY-SA 4.0, https://creativecommons.org/licenses/by-sa/4.0, via Wikimedia Commons)

Right: When ALI merged with Transadriatica, SISA and Airone, the fleets were reunited, and the airline took the name of ALI-Flotte Riunite (ALI Fleet Reunited). (Jozef Mols collection)

One of Linee Aeree Italiane's (LAI) LAI's Douglas DC-3s carried the ashes of Holocaust victims back to Israel. (National Photo Collection of Israel, public domain)

An old photo of an LAI Douglas DC-3 at the Pantelleria airport, Italy. (Aeroporte di Pantelleria, public domain)

With the introduction of Convair CV-240 aircraft, both seat capacity and passenger comfort were increased. (Thijs Postma collection)

An LAI Convair CV 240. (Thijs Postma collection)

An LAI Douglas DC-6B. (Thijs Postma collection)

With the DC-6B, it became possible to start up a route to New York. (Thijs Postma collection)

An LAI Vickers Viscount. (ETH Library Zürich, public domain)

LAI was the first Italian airline to introduce such modern equipment. (Thijs Postma collection)

Alitalia used the Lancastrian on its route to South America. (Thijs Postma collection)

Besides the Lancastrians, Alitalia also operated some Fiat G.12 aircraft. (Thijs Postma collection)

When Alitalia modernised its fleet, Douglas DC-3 aircraft were obtained. (Alan Bushell collection)

Convair 340s were also added to the fleet. (Alan Bushell collection)

An Alitalia Convair 340 in flight. (Thijs Postma collection)

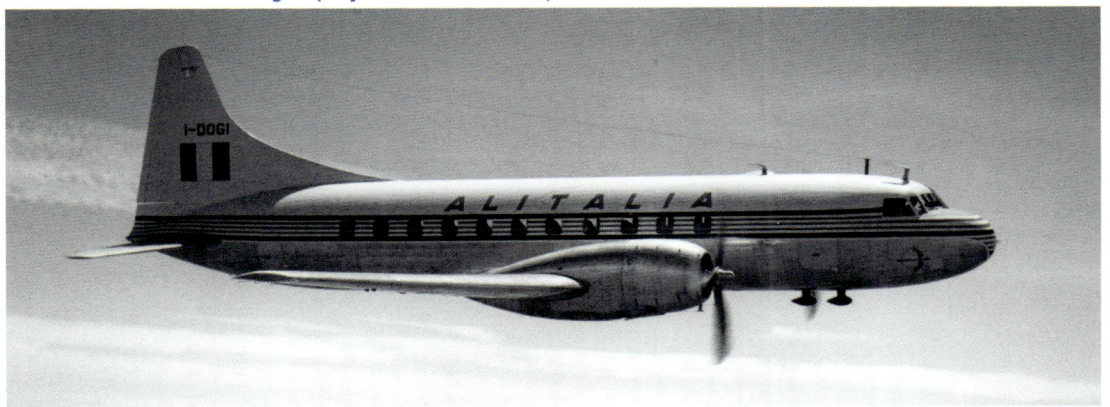

Above: With the introduction of the Douglas DC-6, long-haul routes could be inaugurated. (Alan Bushell collection)

Left: An Alitalia Douglas DC-6 in flight. (Thijs Postma collection)

Below: Besides the DC-6, Alitalia also obtained some Douglas DC-4 aircraft. (Jozef Mols collection)

Chapter 4
The Merger

On 31 October 1957, the IRI, which controlled both LAI and Alitalia Aerolinea Italiane Internazionale, imposed the merger of the two airlines, thus consolidating the Italian air transport market. The new company would continue to use the name Alitalia and was based at Rome Ciampino airport. The capital of the new company was divided as follows: 82.7 per cent for IRI, 6.07 per cent for the Ministry of State Participations, 4.5 per cent for BEA, 2.25 per cent for British Overseas Airways Corporation (BOAC), 3.5 per cent for Fiat, and the remaining shares in the hands of several Italian private companies. Aerolinea Italiane Internazionale had a fleet of 37 aircraft, including six former LAI Viscount 700s, which were transferred to Alitalia as a result of the merger.[1] A year later, the airline would add another four of these aircraft and, in the meantime, new DC-7Cs had been obtained in late 1957.[2] Former Aerolinea Italiane Internazionale Convair 340s were converted to Convair 440 specifications. The merger took Alitalia from 20th to 12th place in the large international carriers' ranking, with a network of roughly 62,000 miles (100,000km).[3] By the end of 1957, the airline had transported over 478,000 passengers.[4]

The year 1960, during which the Rome Olympics were organised, was a milestone for Alitalia. Chosen as the official carrier for the Games, the company introduced the first jet airliners. French Caravelle SE 210s would serve medium-haul routes. The first Caravelle (I-DAXA) was introduced on the Rome–London route on 23 May 1960. It was the first of 14 ordered aircraft, but Alitalia would only receive four Caravelle IIIs as later aircraft were upgraded to Caravelle VI-N configuration before delivery. The last Caravelle was delivered in 1966. Four larger Conway-powered Douglas DC-8-42s were put into service on intercontinental routes. They would soon be followed by 11 DC-8-43s. These additions to the Alitalia inventory helped the airline achieve its goal of carrying one million passengers in one year, and the Douglas DC-8 would become the backbone of the carrier's long-haul fleet throughout the 1960s.[5] One year after the introduction of jet aircraft, Alitalia would move its operational base from Rome Ciampino to the new Leonardo da Vinci International Airport at Fiumicino (more commonly known as Rome Fiumicino). In order to train the pilots of the rapidly expanding airline, Alitalia ordered some Aermacchi MB-326D aircraft, which would remain in service from 1963 until 1967.

In the meantime, Alitalia had also relaunched the pre-war SAM as a non-International Air Transport Association (IATA) Alitalia subsidiary to operate Inclusive Tour flights (whereby tickets can only be sold together with land services, such as hotel or car rental), together with local cargo and secondary domestic passenger services on behalf of the parent company.[6] Alitalia participated in the capital of the new airline for 80 per cent of the shares. While Alitalia had moved its operations to Rome Fiumicino, SAM would operate its charter flights from the Ciampino airport. SAM started up its services with three Douglas DC-6B aircraft obtained from Alitalia, with the first being delivered on 1 April 1961. Alitalia also decided to transfer several domestic routes to SAM. For that purpose, former Douglas DC-3s were transferred from the Alitalia inventory to SAM.[7] In 1962, SAM purchased two second-hand Curtiss C-46 Commandos from the Boreas Corporation to be used on cargo flights on behalf of Alitalia. The flights were operated as feeder operations for Alitalia's cargo flights to New York, operated by a Douglas DC-7CF. Besides flowers, these aircraft would also transport spare parts for Fiat and Maserati to dealers in Europe and the US. As 1962 was a good year for SAM, Alitalia transferred two more

Douglas DC-6Bs to the subsidiary. These aircraft were not only used to fly tourists to destinations like Nice in France, but also to bring ship crews to destinations as far away as Hong Kong. The United Kingdom was a major market for SAM, and it brought 25,000 British passengers to the Italian beaches in 1962. Long-haul charter flights were operated to Tokyo, Johannesburg and Perth. In the early sixties, most charter airlines used Vickers Vikings and Douglas DC-3 and DC-4 aircraft in a high-density cabin layout. Flying in a SAM DC-6B with 85 seats in a comfortable pressurised cabin was a lot more pleasant. Travel organisations such as Club Méditerranée were therefore eager to offer their clients SAM flights to their holiday resorts.[8]

By 1963, SAM needed most of its capacity to operate its successful charter flights. Its parent company Alitalia therefore decided to set up another airline, Aero Trasporti Italiani or ATI, to take over secondary domestic routes in southern Italy that were previously operated by SAM.[9] Alitalia was the major shareholder with 90 per cent of ATI's capital with the remaining 10 per cent held by the state holding company IRI (which also remained the major shareholder of Alitalia itself). ATI started its operations on 2 June 1964 from its headquarters and main hub at the Naples Capodichino airport with a pair of Fokker F27s, of which a total of 13 would be delivered by 1969. That same year, the first four Douglas DC-9-32s would join ATI's fleet. Initially, ATI would fly the Trieste–Venice–Florence–Rome, Rome–Naples–Palermo–Trapani–Pantelleria, Palermo–Catania–Regio Calabria–Naples–Rome and Rome–Grosseto–Milan routes.[10]

As ATI had taken over some routes from SAM, SAM could sell its ageing Douglas DC-3 fleet. Most of these aircraft would be sold to African carriers. In the meantime, the last Douglas DC-6B was added to the SAM fleet. Besides charter flights from European destinations to Italy, SAM increased its presence in the market for long-distance flights with operations to Australia and Canada. In 1967, the carrier entered the lucrative cruise business when it started operating flights from Venice for the Greek Chandris Line, followed by charter flights for Lauro Lines and Lloyd Triestino, which operated cruises from Genoa.[11] ATI on the other hand signed an agreement with Kingdom of Libya Airlines on 15 June 1966. As a result, ATI would run domestic routes in Libya and weekly flights to Malta, Tunis and Cairo with its Fokker fleet. In 1966, the Sardinia region was added to ATI's network when the fleet reached seven F27s and the airline transported 300,000 passengers. In 1967, ATI also took over the management of Elivie, another Alitalia subsidiary, but ceased its existing helicopter operations in 1971.[12]

Besides setting up subsidiaries, Alitalia had been busy expanding its own business as well. In 1965, the airline obtained a 49 per cent participation in Somali Airlines, followed in 1967 by a 40 per cent participation in Air Zambia. By 1967, Alitalia had become the third largest airline in Europe with a network serving 70 countries and a work force of over 10,000 people.[13] The same year, when the new tricolored 'A' appeared on the tail fins of its aircraft for the first time, Alitalia purchased several DC-9-32s for its medium-haul routes in Europe and the Middle East. At nearly the same time, nine extreme-range Douglas DC-8-62s were obtained. The following year, with the retirement of the ageing Viscount fleet, Alitalia had completed the transformation into an all-jet fleet with 19 DC-8s, 24 DC-9s and 19 Caravelles.[14]

The introduction of the Douglas DC-9 resulted in the transfer of Alitalia's Caravelles to SAM. In 1968, the first three SE-210s entered the SAM fleet. In turn, SAM could ground its DC-6 fleet. But these aircraft were not sold. Instead, they were converted for cargo transportation. This way, they could replace the Curtiss C-46 Commandos, and, interestingly, would also be used to transport racehorses, a lucrative business. The freighter conversion of the DC-6s was executed by Alenia Engineering in Venice. The two Curtiss Commandos were sold to Aaxico Sales in Miami to finally end up with Hank Wharton's North American Trading Company, which would use the aircraft on cargo flights in Africa.

As a result of the merger with LAI, Alitalia added some Viscounts to its fleet. (Ken Fielding, https://www.flickr.com/photos/kenfielding, CC BY-SA 3.0, https://creativecommons.org/licenses/by-sa/3.0, via Wikimedia Commons)

An Alitalia Viscount in flight on a European route. (Thijs Postma collection)

When Italy hosted the Olympic Games in 1960, Alitalia introduced the Caravelle. (Jozef Mols)

An Alitalia Caravelle taking off from Zürich Kloten Airport. (ETH-Bibliothek Zürich, Bildarchiv/Stiftung Luftbild Schweiz)

An old postcard, issued by the airline, showing its Caravelle. (Alitalia/Jozef Mols collection)

For its long-haul services, Alitalia added the Douglas DC-8 to its fleet, like this DC-8-43. (Thijs Postma collection)

Above: Alitalia obtained both Douglas DC-8-43 and Douglas DC-8-42 jets. The latter depicted in this image. (Alan Bushell)

Left: A Douglas DC-8-43. The Douglas jets would remain the backbone of Alitalia's long-haul fleet for a long time. (Jozef Mols)

Below: A Douglas DC-8-43 seen in flight. (Thijs Postma collection)

The Douglas DC-8-62 joined the fleet a little bit later. (Alan Bushell)

SAM received the Douglas DC-6B from its parent company Alitalia. (Ken Fielding, https://www.flickr.com/photos/kenfielding, CC BY-SA 3.0, https://creativecommons.org/licenses/by-sa/3.0, via Wikimedia Commons)

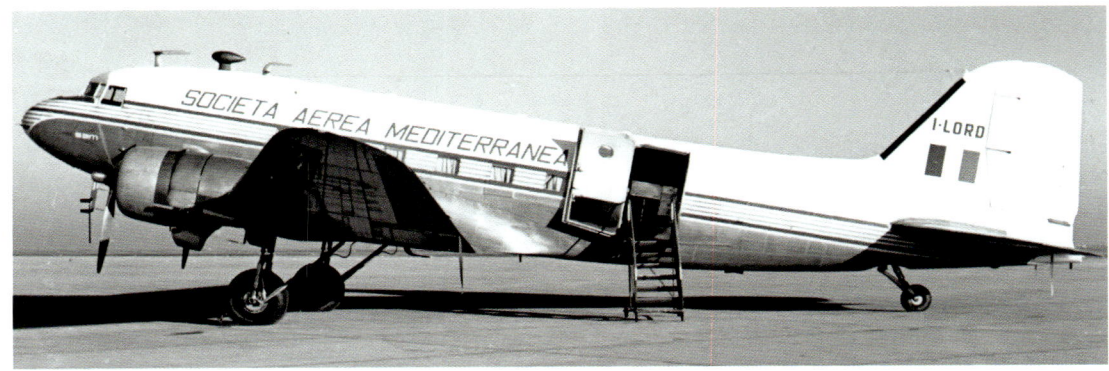

SAM also obtained some Douglas DC-3s from the Alitalia inventory. (Jozef Mols collection)

To operate cargo feeder services for Alitalia, SAM bought two second-hand Curtiss C-46 aircraft. (Thijs Postma)

For its charter operations, SAM used the Caravelle, most of them on loan from Alitalia. (Ken Fielding, https://www.flickr.com/photos/kenfielding, CC BY-SA 3.0, https://creativecommons.org/licenses/by-sa/3.0, via Wikimedia Commons)

When Alitalia adopted the 'A' logo on its tail, SAM did the same. (Alan Bushell)

ATI, which was set up to operate domestic flights, operated a fleet of Fokker F-27 Friendships. (Thijs Postma)

Jet pilots were trained with this Aermacchi MB-326D from 1963 until 1967. (Walter Gori, public domain, via Wikimedia Commons)

Douglas DC-9-32 jets entered the fleet by the end of the 1960s. (Aero Icarus from Zürich, Switzerland, CC BY-SA 2.0, https://creativecommons.org/licenses/by-sa/2.0, via Wikimedia Commons)

Chapter 5
Troubles Ahead

During the late 1960s and early '70s, dramatic developments took place in the aerospace industry. In 1969, Boeing introduced the Boeing 747 'Jumbo Jet'. The aircraft had virtually twice the passenger capacity of the airline's existing aircraft, promising an increase in revenue for the airlines. And in the same period, the demand for air transportation had doubled as a result of new social benefits such as paid holidays for workers. Alitalia responded to this demand by placing an order for the Jumbo Jet. Two 747-100s were delivered in 1970, followed by two 747-200s in 1971 and another 747-200 in 1972. The first 747-100 entered commercial service in May 1970. The type would mainly be used on the north Atlantic routes. In June 1970, in order to expand its widebody fleet, Alitalia also ordered the Douglas DC-10-30. Four of these jets were delivered in 1973, followed by two more in 1974 and the last two in 1975. Despite the availability of these large jets, Douglas DC-8s could still be found on the majority of the extensive long-range network, which at the time stretched all the way to Australia (via several stops in Asian countries). The DC-8-62s were, by then, primarily used on the impressive South American network; those included services from Milan Linate to Buenos Aires, Montevideo, Rio de Janeiro, Sao Paulo and Santiago, and from Rome to Caracas and Lima. The 62 was also used on routes to Chicago, Johannesburg, Philadelphia and Tehran. The DC-8-43 was used on the North African network and operated high-density European (and even domestic) routes. This would last until 1976, when the DC-8s would be gradually retired.[1]

During the 1970s, Alitalia experienced increasingly difficult financial circumstances. The price of crude oil quadrupled as a result of the first oil crisis, and, due to this, Western economies entered a period of recession and airlines experienced a sharp decrease in demand. One solution was to furnish the fleet with more fuel-efficient aircraft. Alitalia's gas-guzzling DC-8s and Caravelles would have to go.[2] Many Caravelles were transferred to SAM, which in 1972 operated a fleet of eight Alitalia jets. By 1973, SAM transported 687,000 passengers.[3] In the meantime, the airline had requested landing rights in the United States. It was the intention to operate such flights with a Douglas DC-8-43 on loan from Alitalia, but the project never materialised. As previously mentioned, SAM had been incorporated as a non-IATA subsidiary of Alitalia. The IATA had imposed minimum airline fares on all sectors flown by its members, but as SAM was not an IATA member, it could undercut such minimum fares and offer tickets at lower prices. Under pressure from the American branch of IATA, the organisation decided to deregulate the market, meaning minimum fare requirements would no longer be imposed. It was therefore no longer necessary for Alitalia to keep SAM as a non-IATA branch to undercut prices. By the end of 1974, the SAM fleet was reduced to three Caravelles. Two of them were painted with the new Alitalia livery. When the last Caravelles left the Alitalia fleet in 1977, this was also the end of SAM's operations[4], and in 1981 Alitalia decided to liquidate SAM.

The replacement of the fuel-inefficient Caravelles and older Douglas DC-8-43 jets had become a top priority for Alitalia following the drastic increase in oil prices as a result of the oil crisis of 1973.[5] Whereas Boeing 747s and DC-10-30s had rejuvenated the long-distance fleet, Caravelles and the old DC-8-43s were still used on medium-haul and European routes. Of course, Alitalia had introduced 47 DC-9-32s, which were spread amongst Alitalia itself and its ATI subsidiary, but the remainder of these smaller jets were made up of the older types.[6] So, Alitalia undertook a competitive bid between the new Airbus A300 widebody, the Douglas DC-9-51 and the Boeing 727-200 Advanced. Boeing won the order, primarily because Boeing was indeed willing to take seven DC-8-43s in part payment for the new order. The Douglas DC-9-50 lost out because it needed the JT8D-17 engine (and therefore lost commonality with the DC-9-32s already in Alitalia's fleet), and it lacked the necessary range to replace the Douglas DC-8-43. And besides, at that time, the Italian aerospace industry was working together with Boeing on the development of the projected Boeing 7X7. As a result, seven Boeing 727-200s began to arrive in 1976, and a further 11 would be purchased in 1978/79. These aircraft were used on European, Middle Eastern and African routes. Some of them had a dual class configuration, others had a high-density 161 seat configuration to serve on domestic routes.

However, by the time the last 727s arrived in Italy, Alitalia had already signed an agreement for the purchase of the Airbus A300, and the Boeings would only remain in service for a short period of time. Indeed, in 1982, Alitalia accepted an offer from McDonnell Douglas to replace its 727s completely with the new MD-80s: a daring move, considering Alitalia had only accepted the last 727s the previous year. But the 727 was a popular aircraft, so Alitalia easily sold 16 of them to startup US airline PEOPLExpress.[7] At the same time, Alitalia considered selling off its DC-10-30 fleet over security concerns after several accidents involving aircraft serving with other airlines. In exchange, the airline was planning to obtain more Boeing 747s of the Combi type, which would allow for more flexibility in passenger and cargo transport. In 1982, Alitalia transported – for the first time – more than ten million passengers and the airline opened a flight school in Alghero. Around this time, the first Airbus A300's also entered the fleet.

Inflation and political instability in Italy during the second half of the decade, however, left the airline facing large debts, persistent losses and falling revenues.[8] Notwithstanding the increased fuel costs, the Italian government, a shareholder in Alitalia via the IRI, refused to allow an increase in domestic fares. Instead, Alitalia was compensated with a subsidy of US$10m per year. In late 1980, the private domestic carrier Itavia had gone out of business. In response, Alitalia and ATI set up Aermediterranea to replace the defunct carrier. Alitalia provided 55 per cent of the capital and ATI provided the remaining 45 per cent. The entire flight crew of Itavia was transferred to Aermediterranea. The airline would enter service on 1 July 1981, using eight McDonnell Douglas DC-9-32s on loan from Alitalia. In 1982, the carrier had transported 572,000 passengers, but later, in 1985, Aermediterranea ceased to exist, and its employees and aircraft were transferred over to ATI.

In order to maximise its potential for profit, Alitalia began to diversify its operations by creating separate support companies that would provide travel services and information. These included Società Italiana Gestione Sistemi Multi Accesso (SIGMA), which focused on the development and management of information services in the tourist sector; Italiatours, which promoted tourism in Italy; and Alidata, a software marketing company.[9]

During the first half of the 1980s, Alitalia went through a substantial restructuring at the hands of Luciano Sartoretti, the managing director of finance who had been in charge since 1979. By 1986, he had trimmed and reshaped the company's debts. In 1987, Alitalia returned a profit of over L73bn following a period of healthy expansion across much of the European airline industry notwithstanding the oil crisis, economic recession and political instability in Italy. But the airline still had to face several problems. Although the company's performance was considered to be adequate, it was losing market share both within Europe and on the transatlantic routes. Air France and Lufthansa were its closest competitors. They had been pursuing aggressive expansion plans through major re-equipment programmes and allowing for greater passenger capacity on profitable routes. Alitalia, on the other hand, had spent its time diversifying its interests and had failed to expand its fleet. The airline had therefore been unable to benefit from a number of generally profitable years in the airline business of the 1980s.[10]

Just like Alitalia, ATI operated a fleet of Douglas DC-9-32s. (Alan Bushell)

The Douglas DC 9 was delivered to Alitalia in October 1967 and was used until 1994. (Jozef Mols)

Boeing 727s replaced the Caravelle fleet. (Kambui, CC BY 2.0, https://creativecommons.org/licenses/by/2.0, via Wikimedia Commons)

The Boeing 727 entered Alitalia's fleet in 1977 and would serve the airline until 1985. (Thijs Postma)

Another Alitalia Boeing 727-200. (Alan Bushell)

Boeing 747-200s were obtained for the long-haul fleet. (Jozef Mols)

The Douglas DC-10-30 was added to the long-haul fleet. (Alan Bushell)

In an unexpected move, Alitalia decided to replace its Boeing 727s with McDonnell Douglas Super 80s. (Jozef Mols)

When Itavia went out of business, Alitalia and ATI together set up Aermediterranea. (Alan Bushell)

In the early 1980s, the Airbus A300 also joined the fleet. (Alan Bushell)

Chapter 6
The 1990s

Although Alitalia had returned to profitability in 1987, this did not mean the airline was out of troubled waters. Beginning in September 1987, Alitalia was plagued with a series of disruptive strikes by pilots, cabin staff and ground crew. This reflected not only senior management's inability to deal effectively with its employees in the short-term, but also the general weakness in their long-term planning.[1] Alitalia recruited Carlo Verri from the executive committee of the Swedish Electrolux AB group, who had no previous experience in the airline business. His task was to provide Alitalia with free market know-how and top management expertise. Of course, Verri first wanted to resolve the labour problems. In May 1989, he reached an agreement with the cabin crew for a 20-month period, followed in July by a four-year agreement with the pilots. Once this problem was solved, he announced a plan to finance a long-term re-equipment programme for both aircraft and ground equipment.[2] When Verri was killed in an automobile accident in November 1989, he was replaced by Giovanni Bisignani.

In the meantime, Alitalia had invested in Avianova, an airline set up in Sardinia in 1986, which operated a fleet of Saab 340, Jetstream 31 and ATR-42 aircraft. Due to this investment, the airline became part of the Alitalia Group. Once Alitalia had invested in the carrier, Avianova also obtained Fokker 70 and ATR-72 equipment. In 1990, Avianova in turn acquired Aliblu, another small regional carrier.

Inevitably, the war in the Persian Gulf in 1991 interrupted Alitalia's routes in the Mediterranean and the Middle East. Nevertheless, aggressive marketing and competitive pricing in 1991 resulted in unexpectedly good results, including a 5.3 per cent growth in cargo operations against an average decrease of 2.7 per cent for other European national carriers. Alitalia briefly participated in an innovative 'air bridge', shipping bodies built by Italian car design firm Pininfarina for the short-lived Cadillac Allanté from Turin to Detroit. Despite these good results, the airline had to post a loss in 1991, just like everyone else in the business. By the end of the year, the carrier employed nearly 20,000 people, and the Alitalia Group had a workforce of nearly 30,000.[3]

The same year, Alitalia introduced the McDonnell Douglas MD-11 on its long-distance flights, which made it possible for passengers to fly direct over 12,000km (7,460 miles). This was the first step in an ambitious five-year investment plan calling for a huge expansion of the Alitalia fleet to 165 aircraft. According to Giovanni Bisignani, the expansion plan was designed to enable the airline to survive by 'moving to achieve a critical mass but staying fast and flexible'.[4] In December 1992, Alitalia entered into an equity partnership with Hungarian carrier Malev. The £61.4m (US$ 77m) investment gave 30 per cent of Malev to Alitalia and five per cent to the Italian government unit SIMEST S.p.A. The expectation was to develop Budapest as a gateway between Eastern and Western Europe and to feed passengers from Eastern Europe into the Alitalia long-distance flights. In the same period, Giorgio Armani designed the new uniforms for the staff and also helped with the cabin design amid the launch of the carrier's frequent flyer programme Mille Miglia. By 1993, the airline transported 38.7 per cent of all international passengers on flights from Italy and had become the third largest European company after Lufthansa and British Airways. That year, however, Alitalia also lost £162m (US$203m). As a result, the new Alitalia CEO, Roberto Schisano, had to cut 1,500 jobs while his company was struggling with debts of £1.43bn (US$ 1.8bn). In 1994, the first Airbus A321 entered the fleet for use on medium-range routes. That year, Alitalia transported some 20 million passengers. By 1995, Alitalia transported 50 per cent of all Italians who took aircraft to fly to their destinations.[5]

In 1993, Alitalia had started talks with Air France. These negotiations were interrupted by workers unrest at the French airline, which would result in the resignation of its CEO, Bernard Attali. While the talks with Air France were halted, Alitalia inked a lucrative marketing deal with Continental Airlines from the US. Although deregulation in the US resulted in the creation of many new airlines, including low-cost carriers, Alitalia had not been prepared for the impact of deregulation in Europe. The carrier saw many competitors enter the market, many of which were budget airlines. In 1994, Alitalia took over its ATI subsidiary completely for economic reasons. Although officially part of the Alitalia fleet, several ATI MD-82s would continue to fly in the ATI livery with the exception of the lettering, which was identical to the Alitalia logo.[6] Several factors, including increased competition and lower ticket prices, resulted in a loss of L528bn (£240m) for the year 1994.[7] And things would even get worse. In November 1995, an ambitious regional start-up began competing with Alitalia on the Milan–Rome route. Air One was one of many budget carriers launched on the wings of the economical Boeing 737, although it was the first operator of that type in Italy.[8]

In 1996, as a reaction to the entrance of low-cost carriers in the market, Avianova was renamed Alitalia Team and became the low-cost carrier of the group. It would finally merge into the parent group in 2002. The creation of Alitalia Team allowed the parent company to renegotiate labour contracts with the trade unions. At the same time, streamlining routes and timetables resulted in a more effective use of the fleet. As a result, labour costs decreased from 27 per cent to 20 per cent. In addition, the number of hours lost due to strikes decreased from about 60,000 between March 1995 and March 1996 to zero by 1997.[9] Additionally, in 1996, Alitalia launched its first website.

New entrants on the Italian scene, including Azzurra Air (which would go on to be an Alitalia franchise) and Air Sicilia, lacked Alitalia's access to government subsidies, However, European Union Commissioners, eager to promote a free market, were beginning to place a great deal of scrutiny on bailouts. Tense negotiations resulted in a L2.75bn (£1.1m) recapitalisation for Alitalia in 1997. As conditions for its approval, Europe required Alitalia to divest various holdings, including its stake in Malev. The airline also had to trim operations and lay off 1,200 workers.[10] Part of the recovery package also included the formation of a regional subsidiary, Alitalia Express. After losing £545m (US$ 683m) in 1996, in 1997 Alitalia posted its first profit in nine years of £194m (US$ 243m).

By that time, the Alitalia management was convinced the airline could only survive within an international alliance that would optimise routes and fleet management. Talks were started with Dutch flag carrier KLM, which was considered to have complementary routes with Alitalia. KLM would operate routes to North America and Asia, whereas Alitalia would concentrate on flights to South America and Africa. The opening of the new hub at Milan Malpensa was considered by the Dutch as a precondition for the start of the alliance. In 1999, the agreements regarding the cooperation were signed by both companies as a prelude to a possible merger in the future. The agreement called for the birth of an airline with 300 aircraft, capable of transporting 40 million passengers and capturing 20 per cent of the European passenger market by 2001. This way, KLM-Alitalia would have become one of the largest carriers in Europe. Since KLM had a close alliance with Northwest Airlines, and Alitalia had an agreement with Continental, the implications of such KLM-Alitalia cooperation would run deep as the United States and Italy neared consensus on an 'open skies' agreement. But the project did not materialise, mainly as a result of delays in the construction of the new Malpensa airport. Furthermore, the polemics and rivalry between Milan Linate and Rome Fiumicino airport also contributed to a difficult climate for negotiations. Alitalia estimated the delayed transfer of flights from Linate to Malpensa contributed to a loss of 2.6 million passengers, resulting in a loss of income. This situation, combined with high oil prices and the war in the Balkans, which reduced traffic, caused Alitalia's 1999 losses of over L200bn (£9.5m). Because of the delay in the transfer of flights between Linate and Malpensa, and in the privatisation of

Alitalia, KLM unilaterally cancelled the agreement with Alitalia. The Italian government was supposed to divest its holdings in Alitalia entirely by 2000. This action by KLM in turn resulted in proceedings before the Dutch arbitration court in which KLM was ordered to pay damages to Alitalia in the amount of €250m (£220m). Once KLM had paid this amount, Alitalia could post a profit in 2002. But, in the meantime, Alitalia's CEO Domenico Cempella had resigned from office.[11]

The McDonnell Douglas MD-11 joined the fleet in 1991. (Thijs Postma)

An Avianova ATR-42 in Alitalia livery but with Avianova lettering. (Jozef Mols)

Thanks to Alitalia's investment, Avianova could add the ATR-72 to its fleet. (Jozef Mols)

The Fokker 70 was also added to become part of Avianova's inventory. (Jozef Mols)

Alitalia used the Piper PA-42 Cheyenne IIIA for its flying school. (Jozef Mols collection)

Although part of the Alitalia fleet, ATI's McDonnell Douglas MD 80s continued to fly in the ATI livery, but with Alitalia lettering. (Jozef Mols collection)

This MD-82 was first delivered to ATI, but joined the Alitalia fleet in 1994. (Jozef Mols)

During the crisis period, Alitalia's cargo division outperformed most European carriers. (Jozef Mols)

The McDonnell Douglas MD11 was also used in a cargo role. (Andreagraziadio, public domain, via Wikimedia Commons)

Even the smaller Douglas DC-9 was used by the cargo department. (Alan Bushell)

The first Airbus A 321-100 joined the fleet in 1994. This aircraft, I-BIXN, was delivered in 1996. (Alan Bushell)

When Team Alitalia was formed in 1996, aircraft in the fleet like this Airbus A321 received the red team logo on the cabin. (Jozef Mols)

Even the former ATI jets received the Team Alitalia logo. (Jozef Mols)

Chapter 7
Crisis

The turn of the millennium saw Alitalia start its downward spiral. As discussed, European deregulation created tight competition across the continent, in a similar manner that saw the rise of new players and the collapse of veterans in the United States. Some political leaders considered privatising the airline and, during this era, passenger service began to decline and one could also notice a rise in trade union tensions. The Italian government continued to pump money into Alitalia over the years to support it following labour disputes, and, worryingly, 1998 had been the only year that the carrier reported a profit. Moreover, it would have to report losses of over €3.7bn (£3.3bn) between 1999 and 2008.[1]

In 2001, Alitalia joined the Skyteam alliance with Aeromexio, CSA Czech Airlines, Air France, Korean Air and Delta Airlines. At the same time, Alitalia also started negotiations with Air France regarding a possible merger, but the Berlusconi government would not accept the deal. However, at the same time, the government increased the capital of Alitalia by €1.432bn (£1.278bn). To modernise its fleet, the four-engined Boeing 747s were replaced. An order was signed for the twin-engined Boeing 777-200ERs. But while awaiting the arrival of the new aircraft, Alitalia leased a series of Boeing 767s.

By 2004, Alitalia employed 21,294 people for a fleet of 157 aircraft. The largest part of the shares of the airline were in the hands of the Italian government (62.4 per cent) and private investors, including the staff had a 35.6 per cent share, whereas Air France was holding two per cent of the shares. On the other hand, Alitalia itself had several participations such as 100 per cent in Alitalia Express and Alitalia Team and 20 per cent in Eurofly. Once again, the Berlusconi government intervened by making available a €400m (£357m) 'bridging' loan in order to repay part of the carrier's outstanding debts. In exchange, Berlusconi put Giancarlo Cimoli in as the CEO of the airline. Cimoli was a chemical engineer with no managerial background whatsoever. He had previously 'managed' the Ferrovie dello Stato (Italian State Railway) and had arguably led the monopolist company into bankruptcy. Nevertheless, he received a 'farewell' payment of €6.7m (£5.98m). In 2005, Alitalia's capital was once again increased by €1.6bn (£1.428bn), including convertible bonds of over €500m (£446m), issued with the promise of a return to profit in 2006. Unfortunately, that year ended with a loss of €626m (£559m).[2]

Despite its own financial problems, in 2005, Alitalia offered to take over the bankrupt Volare Group, using the bridge loan of €400m it had received from the government to repay part of its own outstanding debts. Among the other bidders were Air One and Meridiana/Eurofly. Air One went to court claiming that Alitalia could not buy Volare as it had received state aid in the past. The Regional Administrative Tribunal of the Lazio province tried to block Alitalia's acquisition of Volare Group, but the court had to abandon the attempt when it was claimed Alitalia had repaid its €400m loan.[3] In the meantime, Alitalia had created the Volare SpA with the purpose of buying Volare. Once again there were obstacles as the Italian Consiglio di Stato (State Council) backed the acquisition on 23 May 2006. On 2 November 2006, the Regional Administrative Tribunal stated that the administrative procedure used by the Italian government to sell Volare to Alitalia was invalid, but the selling contract was still valid because the administrative court was declared incompetent about this topic. In the end, Alitalia's offer for €38m (£33.9m) was accepted. On 15 May 2006, the former Volare Group employees were transferred to Volare SpA.[4]

As a result of Alitalia's continuing financial problems, the Italian government of Prime Minister Romano Prodi decided to decrease the state participation in the airline by selling 30.1 per cent of the shares. Among the bidders were the AP Holding of Carlo Toto, Texas Pacific Group and Aeroflot. But after eight months, the public offering of the shares was cancelled as the original bidders were no longer interested.[5]

By 2007, CEO Cimoli decided to leave the sinking Alitalia ship; this time, he received a €3m (£2.6m) parting gift.[6] In the meantime, the Italian government had decided it was time to privatise the carrier, as even the treasury was no longer able to cover the airline's losses. In September 2007, the management of Alitalia indicated Air France-KLM would be an ideal buyer for the ailing airline, a choice that was accepted by the government. On March 15, 2008, Alitalia accepted the offer from Air France-KLM. This proposal included a public offer to exchange all Alitalia shares for Air France-KLM shares at a rate of 160 Alitalia shares per Air France-KLM share. Furthermore, the French-Dutch group was also willing to buy all convertible Alitalia bonds. The total value of the offer amounted to €1.7bn (£1.52bn) including a capital injection of €1bn (£892m). Of course, there were also conditions to this offer. Air France-KLM wanted an agreement with the trade unions and the Italian government would have to guarantee Alitalia would keep its traffic rights. Furthermore, the French-Dutch group asked for an agreement with the Rome Fiumicino airport as it was the intention to close the Milan hub and concentrate activities in Rome. Furthermore, an agreement with the state-owned financial management company Fintecna and maintenance company Alitalia Servizi was necessary to ensure the reintegration of maintenance services within Alitalia. Alitalia itself would keep its autonomy and Italian identity, but Air-France-KLM made it clear some 2,100 Alitalia employees would have to go. If the Italian government would agree with these conditions, it would obtain a 1.4 per cent share in the French-Dutch group and the board of directors of Alitalia would have an Italian chairman, to be appointed by the Italian government, for at least six years. The Alitalia fleet would be reduced to 149 aircraft and the new group Alitalia-Air France-KLM would have three main bases, in Amsterdam, Paris and Rome.[7]

By the end of May 2008, Alitalia had become a major topic of debate during the electoral campaigns. Silvio Berlusconi made it clear that, if he were re-elected, he would not continue the negotiations with Air France-KLM. In his opinion, Alitalia had to remain an Italian company. A driving force behind his campaign was that Lega Nord – a right-wing, federalist, populist and conservative political part and one of Berlusconi's most trustworthy allies – were strongly pushing for Milan Malpensa to be the core of Alitalia's operations. The risk for Lega Nord party politicians was the loss of their local electoral support because Air France-KLM was planning for a definitive shift of the core of Alitalia's business from Milan Malpensa Airport to Fiumicino in Rome. But as many experts know, Malpensa has been one of the most expensive failures in Italian infrastructure. It is a huge airport planned with the idea of becoming the most important Italian hub, but built in a foggy valley where the weather is so miserable that, whenever it snows, flights have to be cancelled. Prodi lost the election, and therefore could not sell Alitalia, although just before the political elections in April around 1,000 temporary workers of Alitalia got a permanent contract.[8]

As a result of Prodi's loss, Air France-KLM president Jean-Cyril Spinetta had no choice but to cancel his offer. A few days later, the Council of Italian Ministers decided to grant Alitalia a €300m (£268m) loan to be refunded by 31 December. The European Commission immediately contested this loan and claimed it was illegal state aid.[9] Therefore, the fourth government of Berlusconi converted the loan into shares in the airline.[10]

As the negotiations with Air France-KLM had failed, the Italian government asked the Intesa Sanpaolo bank – which had been a partner of AP Holdings during previous privatisation efforts – to sketch a possible way for new privatisation initiatives. The Italian press anticipated Intesa Sanpaolo would come up with a solution conforming to the Legge Marzano, which regulates the management of ailing or bankrupt companies. On 30 July 2008, Intesa Sanpaolo called for the incorporation of a new company that would take over parts of 'old' Alitalia. AP Holdings S.p.A. (owned by the Gruppo Toto, which controlled already Air One) would be part of the new company. By the end of August, the Alitalia managers examined the financial situation. But as a result of recent changes by the government to the Legge Marzano, the board of Alitalia decided to declare bankruptcy. A few days later, the Rome courts declared Alitalia was bankrupt and Augusto Fantozzi was appointed as commissioner of the airline.[11]

Alitalia Boeing 767-300 in Skyteam Livery. (Brian from Toronto, Canada, CC BY-SA 2.0, https://creativecommons.org/licenses/by-sa/2.0, via Wikimedia Commons)

A leased Boeing 767-300 in full Alitalia livery. (Jozef Mols)

An Alitalia Boeing 777-200 in Skyteam Livery. (Alessandro Ambrosetti from Rome, Italy, CC BY 2.0, https://creativecommons.org/licenses/by/2.0, via Wikimedia Commons)

Boeing 747s were replaced by Boeing 777s. This aircraft, I-DEMF, left the Alitalia fleet in 2002 after having carried the 'Baci dall'Italia' publicity livery for the Perugina chocolate factory since 1997. (Jozef Mols)

Although Alitalia was nearly bankrupt itself, it bought bankrupt Volare. (Jozef Mols)

Chapter 8
CAI-Alitalia

While Berlusconi was arguing Alitalia had to remain Italian, a group of local businesspeople incorporated Compagnia Aerea Italiana (CAI) in August 2008 with the intention to buy the bankrupt carrier. Among these investors were Gilberto Benetton, Roberto Colaninno (president of Piaggio) and Emilio Riva, who was active in the steel industry. The Benetton family would handle its investments through the Società Autrostradala Atlantis, which was controlled by the investment department of Benetton. The same family also had an interest in the company that managed the Rome Fiumicino airport. Besides the Italian parties, Lehman Brothers bank was one of the founding members of the CAI consortium, but it went bankrupt a few months later prior to CAI's takeover of Alitalia. Colaninno would become the president of CAI while Rocco Sabelli, one of his assistants, would become director general. Other investors included shareholders in cruise companies, the steel sector and telecommunications. Not all of these investors were Berlusconi 'fans', but they were convinced the Prime Minister would treat them with favours in exchange for their rescue of the Italian airline. The rescue plan for Alitalia also included a partnership with a foreign partner. Both Air France-KLM and Lufthansa had already held talks with the trade unions to ascertain their support in case their airline would take a 10 per cent share in the new airline, to be organised by CAI. The Italian press speculated at that time that Air France-KLM would favour the Rome Fiumicino airport whereas Lufthansa would rather favour the Milan airport. Of course, the Lega Nord, coalition partner of the Berlusconi government, indicated its preference for a Lufthansa participation in CAI.[1]

Other airlines studied the Italian situation with great care. Ryanair tried to block the possible takeover by CAI by sending a message to the European Union, stating that if CAI were to take over the 'healthy parts' of Alitalia, whereby the Italian state would refund the debts of defunct Alitalia, this would constitute illegal protection of a bankrupt company. If the European Commission agreed with the CAI-Alitalia deal, Ryanair threatened to bring the case before the court of the European Union.[2]

While talks in the 'back alleys' of the government were going on, CAI indicated its intention to buy the 'healthy parts' of Alitalia (including the flight operations) for €275m (£243.4m), and it was also willing to pay €100m (£88.5m) in a mix of cash and debt for other units, and it would take on further Alitalia debts of €625m (£553m).[3] The Italian government agreed to sell Alitalia's assets to CAI at a 'sweetened' price of €1.052bn (£931m). The remaining €1bn (£885m) of debts would be transferred to a 'bad company', and the government would take full responsibility for refunding the creditors. At the same time, the CAI consortium promised to take over Air One, another Italian company which had gone bankrupt. After the Alitalia takeover, Air One would be incorporated within the new Alitalia.[3] This way, the new Alitalia would have eliminated a competitor on the Milan–Rome route on which only competition from the new high-speed train would remain. The bankruptcy administrator fully agreed with the proposals. As a result of the take-over, some 5,000 Alitalia workers would have to leave the company, and their leaving indemnity would be paid by the Italian government. In the end, Italian Prime Minister Berlusconi could assert that he had kept his campaign promise of keeping Alitalia Italian. But as a result of the layoffs, protesting workers cancelled hundreds of flights for some ten days. CAI nevertheless put 12,639 former Alitalia employees to work in the next weeks. On 12 January 2009, at 2215hrs, the last Alitalia flight (AZ329 from Paris Charles de Gaulle to Rome Fiumicino) touched down. A few hours earlier, the bankruptcy administrator had started transferring Alitalia's profitable assets to CAI, which would continue to keep the Alitalia brand label.

On the same day, Air France-KLM obtained 25 per cent of the CAI shares for about €322m (£285m). The agreement with the French-Dutch group included the creation of a European multi-hub system with focus on Amsterdam Schiphol, Paris Charles De Gaulle airport and Milan Linate. This last airport would only be part of the multi-hub system if its role on the Milan–Rome route could be rationalised. Therefore, Air France-KLM requested a guarantee that the highway between Milan and Milan Linate would be finished in time. Rome Fiumicino would, on the other hand, become a main hub for traffic to the Mediterranean, the Far East and Latin America. The agreement also included a paragraph in which the Italian shareholders promised not to sell their shares in CAI for a period of four years, after which they could only sell their shares to other 'privileged' Italians, acceptable to Air France-KLM. The same day, the Ente Nazionale per l'Aviazione Civile (ENAC, Italian Civil Aviation Authority) transferred the air operator's certificate from Alitalia to CAI-Alitalia.[4]

In January 2009, CAI-Alitalia started out with a network that was much smaller than the original Alitalia network. It included six European capitals but with a domestic network equal to 52 per cent of the traffic, which was four times bigger than that of its competitor Meridiana. The first intercontinental flight of the 'new airline' took off on 13 January 2009, linking Milan Malpensa with San Paolo Guarulhos in Brazil. The same day, Air One (now part of CAI) initiated its first flight between Palermo and Rome Fiumicino. The first flight from Linate took off to Naples on the same day. The first European flight linked Rome Fiumicino with Paris. The first intercontinental flight from Rome took place once again on the same day and linked the city with Buenos Aires Ezeiza in Argentina.[5]

By August 2009, the new Alitalia had become the first Italian carrier on domestic routes with a 50 per cent market share and the airline with the third most routes linking Italy with the rest of Europe (before Ryanair, easyJet and Lufthansa). A few days earlier, the board of directors of the new Alitalia had studied the economic results of the first six months of the airline's existence. A total of ten million passengers had been transported with an average load factor of 59 per cent, which was, according to the board, in line with expectations. The total revenue had reached €1.276bn (£1.129bn). These results had been achieved despite a negative global market situation, which reported a decrease of 30 per cent in the first five months of 2009, compared to 2008, with a 40 per cent loss for business travel. In addition to the critical economic climate as a result of the global banking crisis, the first semester had seen the need to completely merge the Alitalia and Air One reservation systems. The board reported a net operational result of minus €273m (£241m). The board also admitted a general scenario of poor punctuality remained on the whole network with an average performance slightly better than a poor 70 per cent. Most of the delayed flights had been operating from the Rome Fiumicino airport, so Alitalia commissioned an integrated project to renew the Rome airport operations logistics, processes and systems.[6]

Chapter 9
New Crisis

Of course, the rescue operation to save Alitalia resulted not only in a change of shareholders: the airline itself would also undergo major changes. The fleet underwent a complete 'makeover'. Airbus A321 aircraft, ordered by 'old' Alitalia, continued to arrive in the CAI-Alitalia's fleet. But at the same time, CAI-Alitalia signed lease contracts for the Airbus A320, of which 54 aircraft would enter the fleet. The first Airbus A320 arrived in January 2009. It was followed in November 2010 by the first of a total of 22 leased Airbus A319s. These aircraft were intended to be used on regional and intra-European routes. Besides, the first of 14 Airbus A330s entered the fleet in January 2009 to complement the medium- and long-haul fleet.

The takeover of Air One by CAI-Alitalia would also result in fleet changes. Air One Cityliner was founded by Air One in June 2006 to serve domestic and international point to point destinations. The first flights had connected Trieste with Rome Fiumicino and Genoa with Naples, and in February 2007, the first international route from Turin to Paris Charles de Gaulle started. When, on 13 January 2009, Air One was absorbed by Alitalia, Air One Cityliner also became part of the Alitalia group with a fleet of ten Bombardier CRJ-900s.[1]

On 26 October 2009, Alitalia could proudly inaugurate its Terminal 1 at the Rome Fiumicino airport, dedicated to national flights, as well as flights within the Schengen area. It was hoped that the opening of the terminal would eliminate previous flight delays in Rome. In November 2009, Alitalia appointed Air France-KLM Cargo as its general sales agent. In December 2009, Alitalia inaugurated four new international routes from the Caselle airport, in cooperation with the Province of Torino, the City of Torino and the Piemonte Region. The new routes would link Turin with Amsterdam, Berlin, Istanbul and Moscow and would be served by the newly acquired Airbus A319. A few days later, Alitalia and Etihad Airways signed a Memorandum of Understanding with the objective of finalising a codeshare agreement, starting in the summer season of 2010. By the end of 2009, the new CAI-Alitalia had transported 21 million passengers and the load factor had slowly increased to 65.5 per cent.[2]

In March 2010, Alitalia decided to transform its Air One subsidiary into a 'smart carrier', in a way that the parent company would be able to diversify its offers in a few Italian regional markets with a demand profile, aimed at low-cost travel. This way, Air One became the 'low-cost' department of Alitalia. In the beginning, Air One would become active at the Milan Malpensa airport in order to counter the entrance of other budget operators at this airport. The airport itself predicted the number of passengers using its facilities would increase from 1.5m to 3m between 2010 and 2012. Air One intended to transport some 2.4m passengers out of this total. Five Airbus A320s would become the backbone of the Malpensa-based Air One operations.[3]

On 7 July 2010, Alitalia signed a codeshare agreement (valid until March 2022) with Air France-KLM for transatlantic routes. It was planned that this way the Alitalia-KLM-Air France group would cover about 25 per cent of the total market on the Europe–North Atlantic routes. The agreement was based on a plan to offer 55,000 seats every day, distributed over 250 flights, leaving from seven hubs, and connecting 300 destinations in the United States and Canada with 200 destinations in Europe.[4] On 22 October 2010, Alitalia signed another codeshare agreement, this time with Indian operator Jet Airways. The agreement would reinforce Alitalia's presence at the Linate airport, but at the same time augment Alitalia's and SkyTeam's presence in the Far East.[5]

All these activities, deployed in 2010, obviously had their cost. The fleet renewal by means of leasing had proven very expensive. On the other hand, demand for air transportation had picked up again after the banking crisis. During 2010, Alitalia had managed to reach a turnover of €3.225bn (£2.83bn) up 14.1 per cent over the previous year. The airline had transported 23.4m passengers, an increase of 7.4 per cent. Nevertheless, the carrier booked an operating loss of €107m (£94m). The increase in passenger numbers had been caused mainly by an increase on intercontinental (+13.7 per cent) and international (+11.5 per cent) routes. The opening of routes to Miami and Los Angeles in the US and to Amman, Vienna, Malaga and Moscow had particularly contributed to this growth. On the other hand, traffic in northern Europe had been disrupted for a while by the Eyjafjallajökull volcanic eruption in Iceland. As a result of the opening of the dedicated terminal in Rome Fiumicino, flight punctuality had reached some 80 per cent. The number of lost luggage complaints, however, still needed attention as it stood at an alarming 10 items per 1,000 passengers.[6,7]

Between September 2011 and March 2013, Alitalia Cityliner took delivery of a brand-new fleet of Embraer 145s and 190s to replace the Bombardiers, previously used by Air One.[8] Alitalia's main fleet on the other hand also saw some changes. Its Boeing 767s, which had arrived as early as 1964, were retired. The last 767-300 flight took place on 27 October 2012 from Lagos (Nigeria) to Roma Fiumicino. A few months later, in December, the airline also said farewell to its last McDonnell Douglas MD-80. These aircraft had been part of the fleet for over 28 years and had transported over 40 million passengers in Italy and the rest of Europe. The last flight, which arrived in Trieste, was accompanied by the Frecce Tricolori aerobatic team.[9]

Earlier, in January 2012, Alitalia had tentatively agreed to merge with fellow Italian operators Blue Panorama and Wind Jet. A memorandum of understanding had been signed with both carriers, and a process aimed at achieving integration had been started. Rome-based Blue Panorama specialised in scheduled and charter services on local and long-haul routes using several Boeing jets, including 767s, 757s and 737s. But the airline was also a possible customer for the Russian-built Sukhoi Superjets. Wind Jet on the other hand used a fleet of Airbus A320s for its low-cost operations and had begun services in 2003 with a strategy to connect Sicily to various points in Europe. According to Alitalia, the integration of Blue Panorama and Wind Jet was 'consistent with the process of continuing consolidation in the air transport sector'. The airline stated the carriers had 'synergistic and complementary profiles' regarding their network and fleet, which could be exploited in a possible tie-up.[10]

In the 2012–13 period, Alitalia also expanded its network by including flights from Rome Fiumicino to Tbilisi, Zurich, Abu Dhabi, Yerevan, Fortaleza and Prague. Also, flights to Oran, Copenhagen, Montpellier, Podgorica, Cracow, Yekaterinburg and Bilbao were added, besides seasonal flights to Antalya and Djerba.[11]

Despite Alitalia's efforts to modernise its operations, the airline was again on the brink of collapse by June 2012, only three years after the previous rescue operation of the 'old' Alitalia. According to Alitalia, the financial problems were the result of international crises such as the currency crises in Greece, Portugal and Cyprus and the escalation of the Syrian civil war. During its three years of existence, the airline had lost €735m (£650m). Air France-KLM lost interest in its partner airline, not only because of the poor results of CAI-Alitalia, but also because of its own financial difficulties. Two options for the rescue of the company were investigated. Some specialists thought the airline could be sold to a leading foreign airline, for example Etihad Airways. Others voiced the opinion that the government, together with private investors, had to provide fresh capital by means of a new shares issue.[12] But none of these paths were followed.

Shortly after being rescued itself, Alitalia absorbed the bankrupt Air One. (Jozef Mols)

The leasing of Airbus A 319 aircraft was part of a complete fleet renewal project. (Jozef Mols collection)

The Airbus A320 was also part of the fleet renewal. This one is seen with the publicity livery for the Jeep Renegade. (Dara Zarbaf)

An Alitalia Airbus A320 in standard livery. (Jozef Mols)

While Airbus A319s and A320s arrived, the A321s – previously ordered by the 'old' Alitalia – continued to join the fleet. (Jozef Mols collection)

One of the last A320s to be delivered to Alitalia. (Alitalia)

Besides the smaller Airbus models for regional and medium-haul flights, the Airbus A330 also joined the Alitalia fleet. (Venkat Mangudi, CC BY-SA 2.0, https://creativecommons.org/licenses/by-sa/2.0, via Wikimedia Commons)

Bombardier CRJ 900 jets from Air One Cityliner joined the Alitalia fleet after the take-over of Air One by the flag carrier. (Aero Icarus from Zürich, Switzerland, CC BY-SA 2.0, https://creativecommons.org/licenses/by-sa/2.0, via Wikimedia Commons)

Alitalia: From Glory to Collapse

An Alitalia Cityliner Embraer ERJ-190 in Skyteam livery taking off from London City Airport (Aleem Yousaf, CC BY-SA 2.0, https://creativecommons.org/licenses/by-sa/2.0, via Wikimedia Commons)

An Alitalia Embraer ERJ-190 in standard Alitalia livery. (Jozef Mols collection)

Alitalia Express Embraer ERJ-145. (Aero Icarus from Zürich, Switzerland, CC BY-SA 2.0, https://creativecommons.org/licenses/by-sa/2.0, via Wikimedia Commons)

Despite its own problems, Alitalia made a bid to take over ailing Blue Panorama airlines. (Jozef Mols collection)

Chapter 10
Etihad

The crisis of CAI-Alitalia was not only caused by international events like the currency crisis in some European countries and the war in Syria. In fact, mismanagement may have been the main cause. The airline had undergone an important fleet renewal programme. But most of the aircraft (77 out of a fleet of 118) were leased, for which the company had to pay £22.26m ($28m) per month. According to experts, this amount was much too high. In fact, Alitalia paid the price of new leased aircraft while it was receiving aircraft that had been mostly made 20 years earlier. The leasing contracts had been signed with 17 different leasing companies, including AerCap, Aergo Capital, Air Lease Corporation, Avolon and CDB Leasing. For 16 Embraer jets, Alitalia paid £3.18m ($4m) per month. For the 42 medium-range aircraft, the airline paid £9.54m ($12m) per month, whereas the 19 long-range aircraft had a price tag of £9.54m ($12m). According to experts, the leasing price for an older Embraer 175 should not be higher than £108,000 ($136,000), whereas a new aircraft of this type could be as costly as £172,000 ($216,000). An Embraer 190 might cost between £119,000 and £203,000 ($150,000 and $255,000), but for each of the leased Embraers, Alitalia paid an average of £199,000 ($250,000). The same calculations can be made for the Airbus fleet. An older Airbus A319 normally lists at £63,600 ($80,000), while a new one might cost up to £ 207,000 ($260,000). For an Airbus A320, market prices ranged between £51,600 and £239,000 ($65,000 and $300,000). The Airbus A321s could be leased for £66,000 up to £102,000 (between $83,000 and $128,000). But the aircraft leased by Alitalia were older models. The A319s were, on average, 11 years old when they joined the fleet, the A320s on average 12 years and the A321s were more than 21 years old. So, these could not be considered new aircraft. Furthermore, the long-range aircraft, which were on average 15 years old, were too expensive, as once again they were leased at prices for new aircraft. Of course, the management of Alitalia, once confronted with criticism in the press, indicated it would 'try to re-negotiate the leasing contracts', using its power in the market as a flag carrier. But by the time the airline started these renegotiations, even outsiders could notice the airline was on the brink of collapse and all bargaining power had gone.[1]

Of course, a crisis of this magnitude could not be solved by appointing a new managing director, so even the appointment of Gabriele del Torchio (previously with Ducati) could not offer a solution to Alitalia's problems. On 3 July 2013, the airline presented its new industrial plan for the period between 2013 and 2016. According to the plan, the role of Air One within the Alitalia group would be redefined, and intercontinental business would be augmented.[2] In October 2013, Alitalia received fresh capital in the amount of €500m (£440m). This rescue plan included a €300 m (£264m) capital increase and a €200m (£236m) new credit line, obtained from a bank that was shareholder in the airline. Poste Italiane participated in the new capital for an amount of €75m (£66m). Shareholders and creditors could only be convinced to approve these measures after Poste Italiane confirmed its commitment, which was therefore crucial for the deal. Without the turnaround plan, the Italian flag carrier could have been faced being cut off by a major fuel supplier, as well as a warning from ENAC that might have grounded the airline. The news of the rescue plan was met with mixed reactions, especially by the airline's competitors. British Airways called on the European Commission to suspend 'this manifestly illegal aid', terming it a protectionist move that undermined competition and favours failing airlines.[3]

In November 2013, the Italian government was trying to facilitate a takeover of Alitalia by Etihad Airways. Informal talks started during a visit of an advisor of the Italian Prime Minister to Abu Dhabi. Several shareholders of Alitalia were present at the same time, which coincided with the Abu Dhabi Air Show. On December

19, 2013, Alitalia officially confirmed that talks were going on with Etihad. Christoph Franz, the CEO of Lufthansa, immediately reacted by stating he was afraid Etihad would turn Alitalia into a low-cost carrier like Aer Lingus. Experts, however, considered the remarks by Franz as a way of undermining Etihad's intentions. Indeed, Lufthansa itself was hoping to catch a large slice of the Italian market should Alitalia go bankrupt. Nevertheless, negotiations between Alitalia and Etihad continued and by early 2014, it was announced a deal was within reach. On 8 August of the same year, an agreement was signed regarding a 49 per cent participation of Etihad in the capital of Alitalia. A few days later, Etihad indicated it would invest €387.5 m (£340m) to take a 49 per cent stake in the ailing airline and also pay €112.5m (£99m) to take a 75 per cent stake in Alitalia's frequent flyer programme. Etihad was also purchasing five pairs of slots at London Heathrow Airport for €60m (£53m), which it would lease these back to Alitalia on an arm's-length basis. Alitalia would undergo a three-year restructuring plan with a goal of being profitable in 2017. More long-haul routes and jets would be added, and unprofitable routes would be cut. Furthermore, the airline's narrow body fleet would be reduced.[4] On 14 November 2014, the European Commission approved Etihad Airways' plans to acquire 49 per cent of the Italian flag carrier. In turn, Emirates agreed to give up take-off and landing slots on the route linking Rome and Belgrade. The Commission, which is the EU's antitrust regulator, had expressed concerns about competition in the Rome–Belgrade route as Alitalia and Air Serbia (which is also owned in part by Etihad) would control the market.[5] For the Alitalia staff there were serious consequences. The Italian carrier would have to end the contracts with 2,171 staff members including 1,590 ground staff, 126 pilots and 420 cabin crew members.[7]

The takeover by Etihad also had consequences for Air One. The airline had to cease operations on 30 September 2014. Destinations served from Air One's bases in Verona, Pisa, Milan Malpensa and Catania were taken over by Alitalia. The entire Air One fleet was put up for sale to cover debts of the parent company.[6] In the meantime, the Italian carrier had signed a cooperation agreement with Air Berlin regarding codeshare flights on routes linking Italy and Germany. Air Berlin would move its flights from the Milan Malpensa airport to Milan Linate.[8]

On 1 January 2015, a new company, Alitalia Società Aerea Italiana S.p.A (SAI), was incorporated as a joint venture between Alitalia (51 per cent) and Etihad Airways (49 per cent). CAI-Alitalia transferred its assets to the new joint venture, including Alitalia CityLiner and the Alitalia brand name. The same day, the first Alitalia SAI flight arrived at Milan Malpensa from New York. The flight was operated by an Airbus A330-200 with the special Expo Milano 2015 livery.[9] On 20 May 2015, it was announced Alitalia would not renew its joint venture with Air France-KLM, which would expire in 2017.[10,11]

On 1 January 2015, shortly after Etihad's participation in Alitalia, this Airbus A330-200 arrived in Milan Malpensa with the special Expor 2015 livery. (Alessandro Ambrosetti from Rome, Italy, CC BY 2.0, https://creativecommons.org/licenses/by/2.0, via Wikimedia Commons)

Chapter 11
Hope in Vain

Etihad's involvement in Alitalia's management was showing its results by 2016. The airline could report it was back on track to become profitable by 2017 and reduced its losses, which decreased from €580m (£503m) in 2014 to €199m (£173m) in 2015.[1] During 2015, the flag carrier welcomed 22.1m passengers, resulting in a load factor of 76.2 per cent. The codeshare agreements resulted in a strong contribution, and Alitalia and Etihad had shared more than 450,000 passengers on their flights.

In part as a result of this positive evolution, and in part under market pressure, Alitalia decided to upgrade the fleet, including new interiors and inflight WiFi being rolled out across all 122 aircraft. In addition to guest upgrades, the airline had given more than 6,000 cabin crew and airport staff a new customer excellence training programme and had created a new guest response team to faster provide more efficient customer service. New operational procedures resulted in an average 80.2 per cent on time performance, while mishandled luggage was down by 50 per cent (in part due to the arrest of many former Alitalia ground staff who had been involved in theft at airport luggage handling centres). Technical reliability had increased to 99.5 per cent. For 2016, the airline was willing to commit €400m (£347m) to fleet, cabins, technology and infrastructure.[2]

The airline management stressed the good results had been obtained despite several challenges. The fire at Rome Fiumicino airport in May 2015 had indeed caused significant disruptions and its estimated cost was around €80m (£69m). Alitalia also had to suspend the Rome–Caracas route due to the Venezuelan government's decision to forbid the repatriation of US dollars from the country. And of course, the Paris terrorist attacks also had a negative impact on traffic.[3]

However, despite the results obtained under the Etihad partnership, Alitalia continued to lose money. In 2016, losses amounted to €500m (£434m). According to Alitalia these figures, published in the Italian paper *La Repubblica*, were not official and the airline indicated that it had no intention of publishing more recent financial results in the near future.[4]

In order to save the airline, a new restructuring was needed as soon as possible. Alitalia's shareholders, including Etihad, proposed a recapitalisation plan of €2bn (£1.74bn). The restructuring plan was drawn up on the traditional idea of shrinking, reducing costs and increasing revenues. By 2019, it aimed to reduce the annual costs by €1bn (£868m), increase revenues by 30 per cent (and thereby gain profitability) and it would have significantly downsized the short haul fleet by 20 units. Furthermore, it would move the short-haul product offering closer to the low-cost competition with buy-on-board, higher-density seating, higher utilisation, ancillary revenues and low one-way fares. At the same time, the plan suggested expansion of the long-haul operations to better serve and regain market share in the Italian market.[5] The plan also included a decrease of all salary levels by eight per cent and the dismissal of more than 2,000 staff members, as well as shorter holidays for the remaining staff. In March 2017, the board of directors of Alitalia approved the turnaround plan. But obviously, the plan had to be accepted by the trade unions. In a referendum for the workers, they rejected the plan by 67 per cent 'no' votes.[6] On April 4, 2017, the airline was forced to cancel 394 flights, including 12 intercontinental flights, because of a 24-hour strike action called by trade unions. Alitalia stated it could confirm that parties would begin talks about the rescue plan with the protesting labour unions. A deadline for the deal was set for 13 April.[7] A few days later, after talks with the trade unions had failed, Etihad decided to end its support for the airline.[8] The carrier from the Persian Gulf was confronted with a near $2bn (£1.62bn) loss at home itself and was not willing or able to continue pumping money into the Italian flag carrier after the negative response from the Italian workforce.[9] 'Without the support of all stakeholders for the restructuring, we are not prepared to continue to invest' said James Hogan, Etihad's CEO.[10]

For the second time since 2008, Alitalia had no choice but to file for bankruptcy, having already cost the Italian taxpayers an estimated €7bn (£6.7bn) since the 2008 restructuring. This would give the bankruptcy administrator the obligation to turn the carrier around within 180 days, sell it or liquidate its assets. With over 12,400 employees the airline was one of the country's largest employers and it operated a fleet of 120 planes. The Italian government ruled out the possibility of a third bailout but gave the flag carrier a short-term lifeline of €600m (£520m) in the form of a six-month bridging loan. 'We wanted to protect ticketed passengers and Alitalia's workers until a suitable buyer would be found' said Graziano Delrio, the country's transportation minister. He also wanted to preserve the value of a company that had such brand legacy and was so important for domestic connections.[11] After the government had ruled out nationalising the airline, it was officially put up for sale.

Apparently, at the end of February, the company had debts and liabilities of €5.3bn (£4.6bn) against assets of only €0.9bn (£781m). In 2014, the airline had sold all its Heathrow slots to Etihad in the 2014 restructuring and its other route rights and landing slots were unlikely to have realisable cash value. The frequent flyer programme Mille Miglia might have had some value, but Alitalia had already sold 75 per cent of this to Etihad as well. The fleet was mostly leased. Alitalia only owned 39 aircraft of its 117 units strong fleet including six Boeing 777s, 30 Airbus A320s and four regional jets.[12] The likelihood of a serious bidder for the business seemed slim. Lufthansa and Air France-KLM, both of whom a decade ago had been interested, had much more pressing matters on their agendas. Ferrovie dello Stato denied rumours that it would come to the rescue. And a non-European bidder would need to find a consortium partner (preferably Italian) to take 51 per cent of the equity.

In the past ten years, Alitalia had allowed its position as the national flag carrier of Italy to erode so much that it had possibly destroyed what may have been a national brand. Its share of seats in the Italian short/medium-haul market had fallen from 31 per cent in 2010 to 21 per cent in the 2017 schedules. The largest carrier in the market was now Ryanair, with a 25 per cent share of the total departing seats. The third and fourth largest were easyJet and Vueling. Long-haul markets had been equally affected. During the 2008 restructuring, Alitalia had moved its long-haul hub back from Milan Malpensa to Rome. Its share of long-haul seats had fallen to 20 per cent of the market, closely followed by Emirates (19 per cent) and Qatar Airways (7 per cent). Capacity on the long-haul had increased by an average of 5.7 per cent per year, but Alitalia's growth had been only 2.8 per cent.[13]

Of course, many of these problems were related to the structure of Italy itself, a country which consists of two or three sub-countries. First of all, there is the north, particularly the Po Valley, which is a wealthy industrial area. The Mezzogiorno in the south, on the other hand, is a relatively impoverished area with regional annual per capita incomes less than half that of the north. Furthermore, while the economic heart of Italy beats in Milan, the political centre is in Rome. Therefore, there is strong demand for airline transportation between Rome and Milan and some demand for flights to Naples on the edge of the Mezzogiorno. This demand, however, was weakened by the introduction of high-speed train connections. The strong demand in the north for long-haul routes is easily diverted to other European hubs such as Frankfurt, London, Paris or Amsterdam. As far as tourism is concerned, visitors prefer direct flights to their holiday destinations, well away from the industrial or political centres and therefore they prefer point-to-point flights by low-cost carriers or charter operators. Considering all these factors, Italy is a very difficult market to operate a flag carrier. Add to this political meddling, nepotism, and corruption and it becomes clear why a carrier like Alitalia had to struggle for survival.

Chapter 12
Government Control

Shortly after the appointment of administrators for the bankrupt airline, the Italian government was said to have received seven expressions of interest to take over the flag carrier. Among them was Ryanair, but the Irish airline had to drop its bid as it was struggling with a shortage of pilots that forced it to cancel thousands of flights. 'In order to focus on repairing this rostering problem this winter, Ryanair will eliminate all management distractions starting with its interests in Alitalia', it said in a statement. The Dublin-based carrier had announced a non-binding offer in July 2017.[1] Italian industry minister Carlo Calenda indicated he had also received an offer from Air France-KLM, but in a statement, Air France said it had not taken part in the process.[2] Wizz Air from Hungary was also named as another tentative candidate.[3] Even China Eastern Airlines was named as a possible bidder after a state visit of Chinese President Xi Jinping to Rome.

The Italian government also indicated easyJet was among the parties that had expressed an interest in the flag carrier.[4] Delta Airlines might also have been in the running. The British budget flyer easyJet indicated it might launch a consortium bid for Alitalia, together with Delta Airlines and Italian Ferrovie dello Stato. But the stance by easyJet remained cautious, as the airline warned that 'there was no certainty at that stage that any transaction would proceed and the airline would provide a further update in due course'.[5] Earlier, Ferrovie dello Stato had been mentioned as the 'preferred bidder' in the eyes of the Italian government as it would put Alitalia under full state control.[6] The railway company had previously stated it was interested in rescuing Alitalia, but only with an industrial partner on board. The prospect of having not one, but two leading industry carriers on board would give the Italian government confidence that the fate of the airline could be saved.[7] The country's right-wing populist government would be inclined to back a deal with Delta and easyJet as long as Ferrovie dello Stato retained a majority stake in Alitalia. The sale and restructuring of Alitalia had earlier been delayed by the change in government in Rome. The involvement of the state-run railway company would go some way to satisfying the party's manifesto promise of retaining a national interest in the airline.[8] For a while, even investment fund Cerberus Capital Management was mentioned as a possible partner for Ferrovie dello Stato as a member of the Delta-easyJet consortium, but the equity firm's interest waned.[9]

A consortium including easyJet, Delta Airlines and the Italian state railway might at first seem odd, but it certainly had its merits. The former, easyJet, was only interested in the domestic and medium-haul operations of Alitalia as these were in line with easyJet's experience. On the other hand, Alitalia's SkyTeam alliance partner Delta was seeking to expand its long-haul interests in Europe and could do so by joining hands with easyJet, whereby each airline would fulfil its ambitions without having to break up Alitalia.[10]

The Lufthansa Group, which had previously been interested in bidding, did not make a revised bid citing the necessity for large-scale restructuring of Alitalia to make the airline a viable option. The German airline consortium's bid had been considered the most promising prior to the Italian general election. According to unconfirmed information from Italian newspaper *Corriere della Sera*, Lufthansa was reported to have offered €500m (£432m) to acquire planes, airport runway slots and air crew. According to the same paper, Lufthansa intended to halve Alitalia's workforce.[11] The strength of employee groups and resistance to restructure operations, however, made a take-over by the Germans less likely.[12] After the elections, Lufthansa ruled out any deal in which the Italian state would be involved. 'Investing is out of the question for us alongside a state-owned entity', said Lufthansa CEO Carsten Spohr. The airline stated to have pulled back after the Italian government balked at the level of cuts at, and involvement in, a restructured Alitalia that the Germans were demanding.[13] In the meantime, while discussions were going on and Italy was gearing up for general elections, the government added a further €300m (£259m) to the loan of €600m (£518m) it gave Alitalia earlier.

In March 2019, easyJet made the decision to withdraw from Alitalia's takeover discussions. It was no longer exploring the possibility of a joint takeover of the carrier.[14] The prospects for the Italian airline appeared to have narrowed just as the stakes were rising. The deadline for firm bids formally ended on April 30, and media reports suggested that Ferrovie dello Stato had requested an extension, to be considered by the Italian government. It was reported by *Reuters* that the railway group and Delta were still ready to contribute a bid worth around €1bn (£860m), but this would still leave a shortfall of some €400m (£345m). The Italian government – it had been mooted – could take a share in the carrier by swapping debt for shares. With efforts to build a rescue package for Alitalia continuing, another issue remained unsolved regarding the €900m (£777m) bridging loans, provided by the Italian government shortly after Alitalia entered administration with the purpose of keeping the airline flying. The European Commission opened an investigation concerning this loan to decide whether it constituted illegal state aid.[15]

Thanks to the bridging loans, Alitalia itself kept flying. Actually, in 2018, the airline was the 12th largest in Europe and carried 21.5 million passengers. As part of its 2018 summer schedule, it operated 4,000 weekly flights to 100 destinations, including 73 international and 27 Italian.[16] The airline's seat capacity had grown from 28.8m in 2017 to 29.6m in 2018. The airline had to cancel routes from Milan to Buenos Aires and from Milan and Rome to Abu Dhabi, but for the most part its long-haul network remained unchanged. Alitalia even resumed a service to South Africa after an absence of 16 years. Competition, however, remained strong, with budget carrier Norwegian offering flights to Fort Lauderdale, Los Angeles and New York. Qatar Airways had ambitions to take a greater share of Italy's long-haul business, operating flights to Los Angeles, New York and San Francisco from Malpensa airport. Nevertheless, Alitalia remained the second largest carrier in Italy on the North Atlantic route after American Airlines. Alitalia's fleet had declined from 101 aircraft in 2017 to 83 in 2018 by reducing the number of Boeing 777s (from 11 to six) and A321s (from 12 to seven). And Alitalia remained the third largest airline in the Italian market after Ryanair and easyJet.[17]

In July 2019, the never-ending saga of the ailing airline seemed to be close to a new chapter. After the withdrawal of easyJet from the consortium, Ferrovie dello Stato held a board meeting to choose among the four non-binding efforts that were received for a 40 per cent stake in a new Alitalia. Ferrovie dello Stato owned already 35 per cent, with the Italian Ministry of Economy maintaining a further 15 per cent and Delta Airlines (which provided technical assistance) with a minority 10 per cent stake. Suddenly, Ferrovie dello Stato announced it had identified Atlantia SpA as the partner to work alongside Delta Airlines on the Alitalia operation. Atlantia was a holding company operating the Italian motorway network, as well as the two airports in Rome, Fiumicino and Ciampino. The main shareholder of the company is Edizione, a part of the Benetton Group. But Atlantia was embroiled in a controversy with the Italian government following the collapse of a motorway bridge in Genoa in August 2018 that caused 43 deaths.[18] The next phase of the process would require Atlantia to present a binding offer by September. In the meantime, a business plan for the new Alitalia would start from a draft already prepared by advisors Oliver Wyman, McKinsey and Ernst & Young. This plan would see the Italian flag carrier develop its hub in Rome Fiumicino. Domestic routes in Italy would be cut back, pushing passengers to the existing high-speed railway network. The focus of the operations would shift to Europe and North

America. New flights would be added to San Francisco and Shanghai, while existing connections to Santiago, Johannesburg and Delhi would be terminated.[19]

While Atlantia was working on its final bid, the Covid-19 pandemic hit the world. The Italian government announced it would take full control of Alitalia in June, adding that the airline would have otherwise gone bust due to the coronavirus crisis. Alitalia's revenues shrunk by 87.5 per cent as a result of the crisis. Stefano Patuanelli, the Italian Minister of Economic Development, indicated that the government would create a new company at the beginning of June that would take over Alitalia completely. He said: 'Thanks to state intervention, Alitalia will be able to compete effectively once the sector recovers from the pandemic.' Later on, the government would decide whether to keep it under government control. He also indicated he would discuss with the transport and economy ministers a possible new international alliance for the airline, once an existing codeshare agreement with Delta Airlines had expired.[20] On 21 May 2020, Alitalia left the SkyTeam transatlantic ventures.

An Alitalia Airbus A 319 seen near Rome Fiumicino. (ERIC SALARD from PARIS, FRANCE, CC BY-SA 2.0 <https://creativecommons.org/licenses/by-sa/2.0>, via Wikimedia Commons)

Chapter 13
New Bidders

After it had become clear that Ferrovie dello Stato had failed to set up a consortium of investors to take over Alitalia, the Italian government decided it would inject €3bn (£2.59bn) into a new state-owned business to save the airline. At that time, Stefano Patuanelli stressed that it was his aim to 'protect current employment levels' and 'he would 'focus above all on long-haul routes, also with new transatlantic alliances'.[1] Almost simultaneously, two new bidders appeared that were also interested in taking over the ailing carrier.

USAerospace chairman Michele Edwards was keen on turning things around for the Italian carrier. Her company was planning a substantial investment and even wanted to operate a fleet larger than the airline's current crop. Furthermore, the company was planning on having one hub for passenger flights and two for freight transport. Edwards pointed out she would be charging 'fair, but not low-cost' ticket prices, with focus rather on families than business travellers. This decision was due to the impact that the coronavirus pandemic was expected to have on travel habits. Nevertheless, she was confident the operation could be profitable after 30 to 36 months. Earlier, USAerospace had already purchased Iceland's low-cost carrier WOW and was drafting plans to start flights between the US and Iceland. It seemed USAerospace had a passion for saving struggling carriers.[2,3]

Besides USAerospace, Colombian-Bolivian businessman Germán Efromovich, former director of the Colombian airline Avianca and owner of the industrial conglomerate Synergy Group, also indicated he was interested in buying the Italian airline. He sent a letter to the Italian Ministry of Economic Development, and also to the temporary administrator who was managing bankrupt Alitalia, to communicate his interest in buying Alitalia outright. He also indicated his willingness to form 'a possible public-private partnership with the government of Italy'. Just like the Italian government itself, he wanted to promote long-haul routes. But he wanted to run the airline, after his investment of at least €1bn (£864m), without political interference.[4,5] In June 2019, Efromovich had already been interested in buying up to 30 per cent of Alitalia and said at that time he 'wanted to participate in the management and restructuring of the airline'.[6] However, Efromovich was removed from the Avianca board for defaulting on a $456m (£369m) loan from United Airlines.

When both proposals were rejected by the Italian government, Efromovich would later take his revenge. In 2022, an ex-consultant of Italy's ministry of infrastructure and transport, Gaetano Francesco Intrieri, launched Aeroitalia, which is economically backed by Efromovich who also became the president of the new airline. On 9 July 2022 Aeroitalia started operating scheduled flights from its base in Forli to domestic destinations, as well as to several European destinations like Malta and Zakynthos with a fleet of four leased Boeing 737-800s and a single 737-700.[7]

Besides USAerospace and Efromovich, an Italian bidder also suddenly appeared. On 15 September 2020, 'ATI, Aereo Trasporti Italiani,' was registered as a trademark. Christiano Spazzali, a businessman and airline consultant from Trieste with a past at Azzurra Air, had paid €101 (£87) and sent document F24 to the office for intellectual property.[8] Of course, there was immediate criticism. ATI had been the name of another Italian airline incorporated in 1963 and had become a registered trademark of Alitalia years later. Spazzali answered that a trademark is only protected if it has been used over the last five years. Since the ATI trademark had not been used by Alitalia for several years, the protection of the mark was no longer valid. The case was sent to the Italian courts and would be discussed for a long time, even after the Italian government had set up a new Italian airline.

On 10 October 2020, the Italian government signed a decree to allow the reorganisation of bankrupt Alitalia as ITA. On 28 October, it was reported that ITA would buy several assets from Alitalia, including the brand and the flight codes of Alitalia and Alitalia CityLiner, a transaction which was expected to cost €220m (£190m).[9] On 8 January 2021, however, the European Commission sent a letter to the Italian Permanent Representative to the European Union calling for Italy to launch 'an open transparent, non-discriminatory and unconditional tender' to shed Alitalia's assets. The letter consisted of 62 requests for clarification, rejecting the idea that the old carrier could sell its assets to a new company without an open bidding. The letter also stated ITA should not retain the Alitalia brand since the brand is an emblematic indicator of continuity. The European Commission suggested that the combined aviation, ground handling and maintenance business should be sold separately to a third party.[10]

Prior to the letter from the European Commission however, the Italian government had already incorporated a 'new' Alitalia. Francesco Caio, an executive with a background in banking, had been named the company's president. Fabio Lazzerini, a former general manager of Emirates, became chief executive officer. The new board had been ordered to start working together with advisors from the Ministry of Finance on the new industrial plan, which would be sent to the European Commission (which was followed by the letter from the Commission on 8 January 2021). Of course, the new airline would have to reduce the workforce of 'old' Alitalia. Unions remained sceptical about the risk of cuts and estimated that between 4,000 and 5,000 jobs would

Efromovich, who once made a bid to take over Alitalia, took revenge in 2022 by starting up AeroItalia. (Colin Cooke Photo, CC BY-SA 2.0, https://creativecommons.org/licenses/by-sa/2.0, via Wikimedia Commons)

be lost. In addition to old routes, some new ones would be added to the network, including several from Rome Fiumicino.[11]

ITA officially opened ticket sales on its newly launched website on 26 August 2021. At the same time, Alitalia announced it would no longer sell tickets for flights due to depart after ITA's launch. A week earlier, the successor to bankrupt Alitalia had obtained its air operator certificate and licence from ENAC. ITA had already announced all staff members would be hired with a new employment contract that would ensure greater competitiveness and flexibility in comparison with other operators in the sector, but negotiations would prove difficult. ITA launched with a fleet of only 52 aircraft, less than half of Alitalia's pre-Covid fleet, and between 2,750 and 2,950 employees, compared with almost 11,000 people employed by Alitalia. As ITA's role had been limited to the continuation of the aviation business, it was hoped more employees could be hired if ITA could win the tender for Alitalia's ground handling and maintenance divisions to be organised in line with the requirements of the European Commission as indicated in its letter of 8 January 2021. The ITA fleet consisted of seven widebodies and 45 narrowbodies. Italy's new flag carrier also decided to launch a distinct loyalty programme because it could not bid for Alitalia's Mille Miglia programme under a deal between the Italian authorities and the European Commission to ensure economic discontinuity between ITA and Alitalia.[12]

Despite its substantial losses, Alitalia managed to sponsor car racing teams. (Tony Harrison from Farnborough, UK, CC BY-SA 2.0 <https://creativecommons.org/licenses/by-sa/2.0>, via Wikimedia Commons)

Chapter 14
Epilogue: ITA Airways

With the creation of ITA Airways in 2020, the 'Alitalia saga' was not yet over. ITA made its maiden flight on 15 October 2021 from Milan Linate to Bari. Just one day before its first flight, ITA was able to purchase the entire Alitalia brand for €90m (£77.67m). This purchase was needed as all the aircraft with which ITA started out its operations were still painted with the Alitalia livery and the uniforms of most of the crews were still the 'old' Alitalia. Had ITA not purchased the brand and followed through with its inaugural flight, the carrier would have faced serious legal trouble. When ITA acquired the Alitalia fleet, there were 52 aircraft (45 narrowbodies and seven widebodies). In just one year, the fleet had increased by 12 units, including Airbus A350 and Airbus A220 aircraft. The first two A220s were painted in the Born To Be Sustainable livery.[1] On 22 September 2021, the airline had announced that it would work with Airbus as a 'strategic partner'. It said it had signed a Memorandum of Understanding with Airbus for the purchase of ten Airbus A330neos, seven Airbus A220s and 11 Airbus A320neos, along with an agreement with Air Lease Corporation to lease an additional 31 new Airbus aircraft, including the A350-900.[2] On 29 October 2021, the carrier officially joined the SkyTeam Alliance, but for the time being only for one year as new owners had to be found and a long-term strategy would have to be determined. ITA was indeed a 'temporary' airline, set up by the Italian government to ensure the continuation of connectivity, but with the purpose of selling off the carrier to national and/or international investors. A week earlier, former Alitalia employees who had not been rehired protested against ITA.

During its first year of operations (from October to December 2021), ITA carried nine million passengers. By the end of 2022, the airline could already announce it had carried over ten million passengers on 97,000 scheduled flights. Nevertheless, the airline had to post a net loss of €486m (£419m) on a revenue of roughly €1.576bn (£1.36bn).[3] The airline emphasised that its 2022 results met expectations and highlighted that the company was still in a 'start-up status' in a market that was still weak after the Covid pandemic. Also, the significant rise in fuel prices following the outbreak of the Russian-Ukrainian war and the value of the euro falling against the dollar influenced the results. But the airline scored well in the regularity of its operations with 81 per cent of its flights landing on time.[4,5]

While ITA Airways took off, the Italian government had to look for investors to take the airline off its hands. As had often been the case during its lifetime, Alitalia's last rites were surrounded by political disputes, with the far-right opposition party Brothers of Italy, blaming Prime Minister Mario Draghi's government for its demise.[6]

While political parties were arguing whom they could blame for Alitalia's demise, candidate bidders were courting the same politicians hoping to be allowed to take over part of ITA Airways. And these were the same investors who had previously tried to save Alitalia from bankruptcy. Indigo Partners is an American private equity fund with a controlling interest in Frontier Airlines plus Chilean low-cost carrier Jetsmart. It also holds a stake in Mexican Volaris and in Wizz Air, which once tried to bid for a participation in ailing Alitalia. In February 2022, Indigo announced it was interested in buying shares in ITA Airways.[7] At almost the same time, Delta Airlines and Air France-KLM teamed up with an unidentified fund to express an interest in a majority stake in ITA Airways.[8]

In the end, however, the Lufthansa Group would be the winner. On 25 May 2023, the Group announced it had reached an agreement with the Italian Ministry of Economy and Finance regarding Lufthansa's minority stake in ITA Airways. Lufthansa AG would acquire a 41 per cent stake in ITA through a capital increase of €325m (£280m) with the option to acquire all remaining shares at a later date. This presented a growth opportunity for Lufthansa Group and a broader access to the important Italian aviation market. As part of the agreement, the Ministry of Economy and Finance would inject a further €250m (£216m) into ITA as part of the capital increase. This way, ITA would become the fifth network carrier in the Lufthansa Group, which already included Lufthansa itself, SWISS, Austrian Airlines and Brussels Airlines.[9,10]

You might think the curtain would have fallen over the Alitalia saga after the Lufthansa participation in ITA, but you would be wrong. On 27 March 2023, while negotiations with Lufthansa were going on – the European Commission announced the previous loans, extended by the Italian government to Alitalia, were a direct violation of European rules. In the past, while under administration by the Italian government, Alitalia had indeed received two loans of €900m (£776.5) and €400m (£345m). In 2021, the European Commission had already ruled that the first loan of €900m was illegal. The European Commission stated: 'Not a single private investor would have given a loan to Alitalia, and the loans extended by the government were a

An ITA Airways Airbus seen shortly after the carrier's first flight. (Marianne Van Leuvenhaege)

ITA was set up as a result of the re-organisation of defunct Alitalia. This Airbus A320 is seen in Germany. (MarcelX42, CC BY-SA 4.0, https://creativecommons.org/licenses/by-sa/4.0, via Wikimedia Commons)

dishonest act by the Italian government which had its impact on national, European and international routes and falsified competition'. As a result, these loans will have to be added to the other debts of Alitalia and will have to be repaid to the Italian government as part of the liquidation procedures. Therefore, the Italian government – as owner of bankrupt Alitalia – will have to refund the Italian government as creditor for the amount of the loans. How this will happen, nobody is quite sure! Italian Minister for Economy and Finance, Giancarlo Giorgetti, regretted ITA was not involved in the discussions with the European Commission.[11]

The Airbus A330-200 used by ITA Airways to transport Pope Francis to Canada. (Khoshhat, CC BY-SA 4.0 <https://creativecommons.org/licenses/by-sa/4.0>, via Wikimedia Commons)

Appendix 1

Incidents and Accidents

(Information from the Aviation Safety Network)

On 18 December 1954, a DC-6B (I-LINE) crashed in New York. The aircraft was flying from Rome Ciampino to New York via Milan, Paris, Shannon, Gander and Boston. During its fourth attempt to land at New York Idlewild, it struck the pier that supported the left row of runway 04 slope line approach lights. The aircraft crashed in flames and sank in Jamaica Bay. Out of the 32 people on board, six passengers survived. The cause of the accident was described as an erratic approach with pilot fatigue as contributing factor.

On 21 December 1959, a Vickers Viscount (I-LIZI) crashed at Rome Ciampino, killing the two crew members on board. The aircraft was being used for a semi-annual flight crew check involving a simulated two-engines out emergency landing. Upon approach to Ciampino runway 16R with engines no 3 and 4 out, it went into a right bank some 400m (1,312ft) short of the runway threshold. The right wing tip struck the ground and the aircraft crashed. It was determined the landing manoeuvre was carried out below the speed limits for safe directional control of the aircraft.

On 26 February 1960, Alitalia flight 618 was a scheduled service from Rome to New York, with a refuelling stop in Shannon. The flight was being flown under supervision of a check pilot. The Douglas DC-7C (I-DUVO) arrived at Shannon without incident and after refuelling, it was cleared to take off. The take-off run was normal, except that it was slightly prolonged. The landing gear was retracted, after which a turn to the left began when the aircraft had climbed to about 50m (165ft). Power was reduced from take-off power to alternate climb power shortly after the turn had been initiated. Following power reduction, the aircraft accelerated instead of climbing and lost altitude while still turning. The left wing struck the stone wall and gravestones of Clonloghan Church, after which the aircraft crashed and was completely destroyed by impact and subsequent explosion and fire. One steward and 17 passengers (out of 12 crew members and 40 passengers) survived. Investigators failed to find any evidence pointing to the cause of the crash.

On 7 July 1962, Alitalia flight 771 took off from Bangkok for Bombay Santacruz Airport on a Sydney–Darwin–Singapore–Bangkok–Bombay–Karachi–Tehran–Rome route. The crew contacted Bombay Approach and received clearance to descend from FL350 to FL200, followed five minutes later by further clearance to 1,219m (4,000ft). While preparing for an approach on runway 27, the crew indicated that they would make a 360-degree turn over the Outer Marker. However, the DC-8-43 (I-DIWD) had descended below minimum safe altitude and struck the Davandyachi Hill at an elevation of approximately 1,098m (3,600ft). Investigation learned that the pilot probably made a navigation error and believed he was nearer to his destination than he actually was. This caused a premature descent in instrument conditions for a straight-in approach to land at night. It also became clear the pilot failed to use the navigational facilities available in order to ascertain the correct position of the aircraft, and furthermore he was unfamiliar with the terrain. All 94 occupants of the aircraft were killed.

On 28 March 1964, Alitalia flight 045 (Vickers 785D Viscount I-LAKE) departed Rome Fiumicino for a flight to Napoli Airport and climbed to a cruising altitude of FL70. Some 22 minutes into the flight, the crew was cleared to descend to 1,524m (5,000ft) and further down to 4,000ft. Five minutes later, the aircraft left the landing distance non-directional beacon for a direct visual approach. A wide turn on the downwind leg caused the aircraft to enter an area of heavy showers. The flight flew into Monte Somma at an altitude of 610m (2,000ft). All 45 occupants perished. The investigators stated a delayed interruption or failure to interrupt visual approach in the absence of minimum visibility conditions required for the type of manoeuvre involved was one of the causes of the accident. They also stated the initiation of the downwind leg was abnormally wide, which brought the aircraft considerably south of the circuit for visual descent to the airport and along an unsafe path in relation to the terrain.

On 2 August 1968, Alitalia flight 660 was destroyed when it impacted a wooded hillside near Milan Malpensa. The Douglas DC-8-43 (I-DIWF) was performing a Rome Fiumicino to Milan Malpensa leg on the Rome–Milan–Montreal route. While descending to the south of Milan Malpensa, preparing for an approach to runway 35, the aircraft entered instrument meteorological conditions with heavy turbulence due to the presence of thunderstorms in the area. Three minutes after the flight was cleared to descent from 2,743m (9,000ft) to 4,000ft for a straight-in approach, the pilot advised that he would make a 360-degree turn over the beacon as the aircraft was still at 1,828m (6,000ft). On completion of the turn at an altitude of 457m (1,500ft), the flight continued on runway heading and descended, but the aircraft had already passed the airport. When, at 14.06, the crew became unsure of their position, the aircraft almost immediately struck a hillside some 11.5km (69 miles) north of Malpensa's runway 35. According to the investigators, 'insufficient checking of flight times during the final portion of the approach' was the main cause of the accident. Also, the positioning of the aircraft for final approach by means of a non-standard procedure, delayed detection of the VHF omnidirectional range (VOR) radial, wrong selection of such radial and broken view of terrain north of the airport similar to that South of the airport contributed to the crash. There were 95 occupants on board of the aircraft. Twelve passengers were killed in the crash.

On 5 May 1972, another Douglas DC-8-43 crashed. The aircraft I-DIWB was operating Alitalia flight 112 from Rome Fiumicino Airport to Palermo Punta Raisi Airport. The aircraft crashed into Mount Longa at an altitude of 609m (2,000ft) on a night-time approach to Palermo. Weather at the time of the accident included broken cloud layers of 3/8 cumulus at 407m (1,500ft) and a visibility of three miles. The official accident inquiry stated the crew did not adhere to the established approach procedures. There is another version of the accident told by some of the victims' relatives. Mrs. Maria Eleonora Fais, sister of Angela Fais, who died in that aircraft, was able to find, after many years, the report of the Vice-Chief of Police Giuseppe Peri that says that the aircraft exploded because of a bombing. Peri attributed an alliance of people having ties with the Mafia and with a subversive right-wing group with the responsibility for this bombing. Three days after the accident the political elections would be held in which a strong rise in Right-Wing voters was foreseen. The National Association of Italian Pilots sided with the pilots, refusing the possibility of a mistake due to their long experience and because the accusation of an intoxication had been denied.[1] Originally, the flight would have carried 132 passengers, but 24 of them did not arrive in time at the departure gate due to different reasons. They escaped the disaster, whereas the seven crew members and 108 passengers on board were killed.[2]

On 23 December 1978, Douglas DC-9-32 (I-DIKQ) crashed on approach to Palermo Punta Raisi Airport. Flight 4128 was a domestic non-scheduled flight from Rome Fiumicino to Palermo. It was an extra service for the Christmas season. The flight from Rome was cleared for a night-time VOR/distance-measuring equipment (DME) approach to runway 21 at the Palermo airport. To approach this airport, the pilot must place the aircraft 16.5nm northeast of the VOR at 4,000ft and then descend in order to cross the 6 DME fix at 1,500ft, the 4 DME fix at 274m (900ft), and the 3 DME fix at 213m (700ft). The latter fix is also the Missed Approach Point where, should the runway not be in sight by this time, the crew should initiate a go-around, turning right on a 332-degree heading, climb to 3,000ft and wait for ATC instructions. The final part of the approach, about two miles, is to be flown visually with the crew having to turn left to line up for runway 21, which had a magnetic heading of 206 degrees. However, on this occasion, the aircraft stopped its descent at about 45m (150ft) above the sea after passing the 3 DME fix. For about nine seconds, the aircraft flew almost level with the sea, then the wind pushed the aircraft and the right wing impacted the water. Twenty-one survivors – out of 129 occupants – were saved by nearby fishing boats. At that time, Palermo Airport was equipped with a primary radar Plessey ACR 430 with an operative range of no more than 24km (15 miles), usable on the North and West quadrants due to high terrain to the East and South, and with no Moving Target Indicator, meaning that there three miles of almost blind spots for the controller. There is no secondary radar capability to give transponder answers to the controller, and aircraft appear as small unlabelled targets on the screen. The accident was attributed to the flight deck crew believing they were nearer to the runway than they actually were, and therefore making a premature descent.

On 30 June 1982, Boeing 747-243B (registration unknown) was flying to Bangkok with a stop at Delhi Palam Airport. On the way to Bangkok, the aircraft was hijacked by a male passenger from Sri Lanka by the name of Sepala Ekanayake. He demanded US$300,000 and to be reunited with his Italian-born wife and child who were in Italy. He claimed to have six accomplices aboard and threatened to blow up the aircraft. Upon landing at Bangkok, he released four passengers. Later, when he learned that his wife and child were on their way to Bangkok, he released about 139 passengers and two more escaped by jumping from the aircraft. After the hijacker's wife went aboard the aircraft and the ransom was delivered, all the remaining hostages were released. Per agreement with authorities, the hijacker and his wife and child, together with the ransom money, were flown to Colombo in Sri Lanka. The hijacker was subsequently arrested by Sri Lankan authorities and sentenced to 20 years to life.

On 14 November 1990, a Douglas DC-9-32 (I-ATJA) operating flight 404 from Milan Linate to Zürich Kloten Airport, crashed on approach to Zürich. When arriving near Zürich, the crew was cleared to descend to 4,000ft and to make an instrument landing system to runway 14. At 14nm from the runway 14 threshold, the aircraft captured the localiser. At about 11.5nm short, the aircraft descended through the cleared altitude of 4,000ft. Descent from 4,000ft was only allowed after intercepting the glide path at 8nm. The aircraft descended about 426m (1,400ft) below the glide path until it struck trees on the Stadlerberg mountainside at an elevation of 506m (1,660ft), at 5.2nm from the runway. The aircraft crashed and broke up, killing all 46 occupants. The probable cause was false indication of VHF NAV unit 1 in the aircraft (due to a short circuit in the system), probable altimeter misreading by the pilot in command and no Ground Proximity Warning System in the cockpit. The pilots were not aware of the possibility of incorrect indications in the NAV equipment in use. Furthermore, non-compliance with basic procedural instructions during the approach also contributed. The copilot's go-around procedure was aborted by the pilot in command, and approach controller did not see the aircraft leave the cleared altitude of 4,000ft before the Final Approach Point.

On 24 April 2011, an Alitalia Airbus A321-100 (I-BIXA) performing flight 329 from Paris Charles de Gaule to Rome Fiumicino with 131 passengers was en route about 30 minutes prior to the estimated landing when a male passenger from Kazakhstan attacked a flight attendant with a nail file and demanded the airplane should divert to Tripoli (Libya). Cabin crew and other passengers subdued the man and a doctor on board put the attacker out of action with a sedative. The aircraft continued for a safe landing in Rome and the hijacker was taken into custody by Italian police. The flight attendant who had been attacked received minor injuries to her neck.[3]

On 2 February 2013, a Carpatair ATR 72 (YR-ATS), operating on behalf of Alitalia, experienced a hard landing because of strong gusty wind at Rome Fiumicino while arriving from Pisa. The airplane flew the approach in strong crosswind conditions with wind shear reported at runway 16L some 15 minutes before the landing. Shortly before touchdown, the aircraft suddenly lost altitude and impacted the runway with the nose landing gear. This was at a distance of 567m (1,860ft) from the runway threshold. It bounced three times, causing the nose and main gear to collapse. The aircraft slid off the left side of the runway and came to rest in the grass at a distance of about 1,780m (5,804ft) from the runway threshold. It stopped 400m (1,312ft) from fire station no. 1. However, it took the fire services ten minutes to reach the aircraft because they were not aware of the precise location of the accident. The accident was due to the human factor. In particular, it was caused by an improper conduct of the aircraft by the pilot in command during landing, not consistent with the provisions of the operator's manuals, in an environmental context characterised by the presence of significant presence of crosswind with values at the limit/excess of those allowed for the ATR 72. All 50 occupants survived, but the aircraft was written off.

On 29 September 2013, Airbus A320-216 (EI-EIB), operating flight 063 from Madrid Barajas Airport to Rome Fiumicino, had a landing accident. While on approach to runway 16L at Rome Fiumicino, the crew attempted to lower the landing gear. A Master Warning sounded and the electronic centralised aircraft monitoring system showed a message 'L/G GEAR NOT DOWNLOCKED'. The crew carried out a missed approach procedure and entered a holding pattern at the Campagnano VOR. A g-force manoeuvre was carried out with the landing gear lever down. When this attempt failed, they tried to recycle the landing gear and then a gravity extension, but all measures failed. Consequently, the crew requested an emergency landing at Rome Fiumicino. The aircraft touched down on runway 16L with the right landing gear only partially extended. The flight crew shut down both engines just before touchdown. The subsequent evacuation was uneventful and there were no injuries. The aircraft was damaged but could be repaired. The cause of the incident can be attributed to the failure of the right-hand undercarriage actuator. There was a hydraulic block caused by multiple debris found within the actuator itself and in the hydraulic fluid. The debris came from two rings found missing from their design position.

Appendix 2
Fleet Details

Alitalia fleet details (based on en.wikipedia.org, planespotters.net and the airline's own figures)

Aircraft type	Total	First introduced	Last removed
Avro Lancastrian MkIII	5	1947	1952
Savoia-Marchetti SM 95C	8	1947	1952
Fiat G 12CA	4	1947	1948
Fiat G 12 LB	5	1948	1950
Avro 652A Anson	1	1948	1949
Douglas DC 4	4	1950	1954
Convair CV-340	3	1953	1962
Douglas DC-6B	14	1953	1970
Convair CV-440	3	1954	1962
Douglas DC-7C	6	1957	1966
Vickers Viscount 745D	10	1957	1971
Vickers Viscount 785D	8	1957	1969
Sud Aviation SE 210 Caravelle III	4	1960	1977
Douglas DC-8-40	15	1960	1977
Sud Aviation SE 210 Caravelle VI	17	1961	1977
Curtiss C-54A	2	1962	1968
Douglas DC 3	13	1962	1968
Aermacchi MB-326D	4	1963	1967
Douglas C-54A Skymaster	4	1965	1968
McDonnell Douglas DC-9-30	46	1967	1998
Douglas DC-8-50	1	1968	1969
Douglas DC-8-60/70	11	1968	1981
Boeing 747-100	2	1970	1981
Boeing 747-200	19	1971	2006
McDonnell Douglas DC-10-30	8	1973	1986
Boeing 727-200 Advanced	18	1976	1985
Boeing 707-138B	1	1978	1979
Airbus A300B4	12	1980	1998
SIAI Marchetti SF 260	7	1980	1997
Piaggio P166	2	1981	1986
Piper PA 42 Cheyenne	5	1986	2006

Aircraft type	Total	First introduced	Last removed
Airbus A300B2	2	1988	1997
Boeing 737-200C	2	1992	1995
ATR-42-300	9	1996	2007
ATR 72-200	12	1996	2013
Dornier 328-110	10	1998	2003
Boeing 747-400F	1	2000	2002
Avro RJ 70	5	2000	2004
Airbus A321-100	23	1994	2021
Airbus A320-200	54	1999	2021
Boeing 767-300	14	1995	2012
Embraer ERJ145LR	14	2000	2009
McDonnell Douglas MD-11	8	1994	2009
McDonnell Douglas MD 82	90	2002	2012
Boeing 777-200	12	2003	2021
Embraer E170	6	2004	2012
Airbus A330-200	14	2009	2021
Airbus A319-100	22	2010	2021
Bombardier CRJ900ER	10	2011	2014
Embraer E190	5	2011	2021
Boeing 777-300ER	1	2017	2021

A Minerva Dornier 328, leased by Alitalia. (Jozef Mols)

An Alitalia Express Embraer ERJ 145. (Jozef Mols)

An Alitalia ATR 42. (Jozef Mols)

Appendix 3
Notes and References

Chapter 1
1. 'Mario de Bernardi', eng.wikipedia.org
2. 'Francesco de Pinedo', eng.wikipedia.org
3. Ibid.
4. 'Italo Balbo', eng.wikipedia.org
5. Siddiqi, Assif, 'The beginnings of commercial aviation in Italy', www.centennialofflight.net/essay/Commercial_Aviation/italy/Tran23
6. 'Società Anonima Navigazione Aerea (SANA)', eng.wikipedia.org
7. Delisi, Bruno, 'Le ali della Rondine: dalle Transadriatica all'Ala Littoria', 2007, www.veniceairportlido.com
8. 'SAM (Società Aerea Mediterranea)', eng.wikipedia.org
9. 'Società anonima di navigazione aerea transadriatica', it.wikipedia.org.
10. Siddiqi, Assif, 'The beginnings of commercial aviation in Italy', www.centennialofflight.net/essay/Commercial_Aviation/italy/Tran23
11. Singh, Bysumit, 'A brief history of the Italian Aviation Industry', www.simpleflying.com, 21 October 2021
12. 'Avio Linee Italiane (ALI)', eng.wikipedia.org

Chapter 2
1. Singh, Bysumit, 'A brief history of the Italian Aviation Industry', www.simpleflying.com, 21 October 2021
2. Siddiqi, Assif, 'The beginnings of commercial aviation in Italy', www.centennialofflight.net/essay/CommercialAviation/italy/Tran23
3. Delisi, Bruno, 'Le ali della Rondine: dalle Transadriatica all'Ala Littoria', 2007, www.veniceairportlido.com.
4. Siddiqi, Assif, 'The beginnings of commercial aviation in Italy', www.centennialofflight.net/essay/Commercial_Aviation/italy/Tran23
5. Sabbadini, Ettore, '30 anni di aviazione civile italiana in Africa', *Rivista trimestrale di studi e documentazione dell'Instituto Italiano per l'Africa e l'Oriente*, year 14, nr 4 (July–August), pp.197–200
6. Alpozzi, Alberto, 'Come l'Italia fascista gesti la posta in Africa', 2017, italiacoloniale.com
7. 'Ala Littoria SA', eng.wikipedia.org
8. Meleca, Vincenzo, 'Le linee aeree dell'Africa Orientale Italiana', ilcornodafrica.it
9. Riccitelli, Flavio, Ala Littoria SA (1934–1941)', www.ilpostalista.it
10. 'Profitability, practicality and ideology: fascist civil aviation and the short life of Ala Littoria 1934–1943', www.thefreelibrary.com
11. Riccitelli, Flavio, 'Ala Littoria SA (1934–1941)', www.ilpostalista.it
12. 'Profitability, practicality and ideology: fascist civil aviation and the short life of Ala Littoria 1934–1943', www.thefreelibrary.com
13. Ibid.
14. Ibid.

15. Siddiqi, Assif, 'The beginnings of commercial aviation in Italy', www.centennialofflight.net/essay/Commercial_Aviation/italy/Tran23
16. 'Avio Linee Italiane', eng.wikipedia.org.

Chapter 3
1. Siddiqi, Assif, 'Air Transportation: The Beginnings of Commercial Aviation in Italy', www.centennialofflight.net/essay/Commercial_Aviation/italy/Tran23
2. 'Abandoned forgotten and little known airfields in Europe', forgottenairfields.com
3. 'Avio Linee Italiane', eng.wikipedia.org
4. Siddiqi, Assif, 'Air Transportation: The Beginnings of Commercial Aviation in Italy', www.centennialofflight.net/essay/Commercial_Aviation/italy/Tran23
5. Petrelli, Marco, "Linee Aeree Italiane: la rinascita del volo commerciale italiano dopo il '45", conoscerelastroria.it, 13 March 2022
6. 'Linee Aeree Italiane', it.wikipedia.org
7. Ibid.
8. 'Rome to organize New York flights: Italian government authorizes LAI to start service', *The New York Times*, 12 December 1949
9. 'History of Alitalia-Linee Aeree Italiana S.p.A', referencesforbusiness.com
10. Ibid.
11. Bertoletti, Mario, '5/05/1947: First flight of Alitalia', airwaysmag.com, 5 May 2022
12. 'Alitalia airlines: Italy's introduction to the world', boeing.com/commercial/aeromagazine/aero
13. 'Aircraft Alitalia: its story lasted 75 years', avionews.it, 14 October 2021
14. 'History of Alitalia-Linee Aeree Italiana S.p.A'. referencesforbusiness.com
15. 'Alitalia airlines: Italy's introduction to the world', boeing.com/ commercial/ aeromagazine/aero

Chapter 4
1. 'Storia di Alitalia', it.wikipedia.org.
2. Stretton, Richard, 'Alitalia-into the jet-age', www.yesterdaysairlines.com, 13 February 2015
3. 'History of Alitalia Airlines – Air One', www.seatmaestro.com
4. 'Alitalia – Linee Aeree Italiana SpA', encyclopedia.com
5. Ibid.
6. 'Società Aerea Mediterranea', eng.wikipedia.org.
7. 'Società Aerea Mediterranea', oud16hoven.nl.
8. Ibid.
9. 'Aero Transporti Italiani', eng.wikipedia.org
10. Ibid.
11. 'Società Aerea Mediterranea', oud16hoven.nl
12. 'Aero Transporti Italiani', eng.wikipedia.org
13. 'Storia di Alitalia', it.wikipedia.org
14. 'Alitalia – Linee Aeree Italiana SpA', encyclopedia.com

Chapter 5
1. Stretton, Richard, 'Alitalia-into the jet-age', www.yesterdaysairlines.com, 13 February 2015
2. 'Alitalia – Linee Aeree Italiana SpA', encyclopedia.com
3. 'Società Aerea Mediterranea', oud16hoven.nl.
4. Ibid.

5. 'I trijets Alitalias 727s', yesterdaysairlines.com, 8 October 2016
6. Ibid.
7. Ibid.
8. 'Alitalia – Linee Aeree Italiana SpA', encyclopedia.com.
9. Ibid.
10. Ibid.

Chapter 6
1. 'History of Alitalia-Linee Aeree Italiana S.p.A.', referencesforbusiness.com
2. Ibid.
3. Ibid.
4. Ibid.
5. 'Alitalia', it.wikipedia.org
6. 'Aero Trasporti Ilaliani S.p.A. (ATI)', eng.wikipedia.org
7. 'L'ati entra nell cabina di Alitalia', Italia Oggi.it, 26 July 1994
8. 'History of Alitalia-Linee Aeree Italiana S.p.A', referencesforbusiness.com
9. 'Alitalia', it.wikipedia.org
10. Ibid.
11. Ibid.

Chapter 7
1. Singh, Sumit, 'A brief history of the Italian Aviation Industry', simpleflying.com, 21 October 2021
2. 'Alitalia', eng.wikipedia.org
3. Ibid.
4. Ibid.
5. 'Alitalia', it.wikipedia.org
6. 'Boykott CAI (Alitalia + AirOne)', gurgleitaly, wordpress.com, 1 August 2009
7. 'Storia di Alitalia', it.wikipedia.org
8. 'Boykott CAI (Alitalia + AirOne)', gurgleitaly, wordpress.com, 1 August 2009
9. 'EU to label Italian load for Alitalia 'illegal' source', reuters.com, 6 June 2008
10. Ibid.
11. 'Boykott CAI (Alitalia + AirOne)', gurgleitaly, wordpress.com, 1 August 2009

Chapter 8
1. 'Alitalia, vola italiano ma a quale prezzo', October 10, racconta.espresso.republica.it, 10 October 2008, (copy of a memo from the American Embassy in Rome to the American Secretary of State)
2. Ibid.
3. Babington, Deepa and Vagnoni, Giselda, 'Update 3 – Italy agrees sale of Alitalia to CAI Consortium', Reuters.com, 19 November 2008
4. 'Storia di Alitalia', it.wikipedia.org
5. Ibid.
6. 'Alitalia Board of Directors analyses the economic trend of the first six months', Alitalia press release. 29 July 2009

Chapter 9

1. 'Alitalia Cityliner', eng.wikipedia.org
2. 'Storia di Alitalia', it.wikipedia.org
3. Di Lino, Vuotto, 'Alitalia: 3 milione di pax a Malpensa con Air One', ttgitalia.com, 11 February 2010
4. 'Storia di Alitalia', it.wikipedia.org
5. Ibid.
6. 'Comunicato Stampa Alitalia-Air One', Alitalia Corporate, 25 February 2011
7. 'Alitalia:Andamento Gestionale 2010', Comunicato del Consiglio di Amministrazione di Alitalia', Italian Parliament, 28 October 2010
8. 'Alitalia Cityliner', eng.wikipedia.org
9. 'Laddio di Alitalia agli MD 80', www.rainews.it, 17 December 2012
10. Kaminski-Morrow, David, 'Alitalia plans merger with Blue Panorama and Wind Jet', flightglobal.com, 25 January 2012
11. 'Storia di Alitalia', it.wikipedia.org
12. Ibid.

Chapter 10

1. Berberi, Leonard, 'Alitalia e il caso degli aerei', corriere.it/cronache, 18 September 2016
2. 'Storia di Alitalia', it.wikipedia.org
3. Riegler, Paul, 'Alitalia secures euro 500million in new funding, avoids bankruptcy', frequentbusinesstraveler.com, 12 October 2013
4. Riegler, Paul, 'Etihad takes 49% stake in Alitalia', frequentbusinesstraveler.com, 11 August 2014
5. Riegler, Paul, 'EU gives greenlight to Etihad's 49% stake in Alitalia', frequentbusinesstraveler.com, 14 November 2014
6. 'Storia di Alitalia', it.wikipedia.org
7. 'E arrivato il si di Etihad, sempre piu vicino l'accordo con Alitalia', corriere.it, 1 August 2014.
8. 'Storia di Alitalia', it.wikipedia.org
9. Ibid.
10. Riegler, Paul, 'Alitalia to end air France – KLM partnership', frequentbusinesstraveler.com, 20 May 2015
11. Frommberg, Laura, 'Alitalia trennt sich von Air France KLM', aerotelegraph.com, 19 May 2015

Chapter 11

1. 'Alitalia reduces losses by euro381mn', aviationbusinessme.com, 1 May 2016
2. Ibid.
3. 'Alitalia', eng.wikipedia.org
4. 'Italy's near-bankrupt airline losses deepen in Q1 of 2017' qatar-tribune.com, 9 May 2017
5. 'Alitalia decline', aviationstrategy.aero, May 2017
6. 'Alitalia', it.wikipedia.org
7. Hofmann, Kurt, '24-hour strike forces Alitalia to cancel 394 flights', airtransportworld.com, 5 April 2017
8. 'Alitalia', eng.wikipedia.org
9. 'Etihad blames rising fuel prices, costly investment as it stays in the red', Reuters.com, June 14, 2018

10. Riegler, Paul, 'Alitalia files for bankruptcy for second time in a decade', frequentbusinesstraveller.com, 2 May 2017
11. Ibid.
12. 'Alitalia decline', aviationstrategy.aero, May 2017 Ibid.
13. Ibid.

Chapter 12
1. 'Ryanair drops its bid to buy ailing Alitalia', thelocal.it, 27 September 2017
2. 'Air France denies involvement in bid to take over Alitalia', Reuters.com, 13 January 2018
3. 'Alitalia's two years in administrative limbo', flightglobal.com, 1 May 2019
4. 'EasyJet confirms interest in Alitalia', aviationweek.com, 15 June 2017
5. Curtis, Joe, 'EasyJet confirms talks over possible bid for struggling airline Alitalia', cityam.com, 14 February 2019
6. Bailey, Joanna, 'Easyjet and Delta in unlikely partnership to potentially takeover failing Alitalia', simpleflying.com, 15 February 2019
7. Ibid.
8. Flett, John, 'Delta and EasyJet submit bids for Alitalia alongside Italian Rail company', airlinegeeks.com, November 5, 2018
9. 'Alitalia's two years in administrative limbo', flightglobal.com, 1 May 2019
10. Flett, John, 'Delta and EasyJet submit bids for Alitalia alongside Italian Rail company', airlinegeeks.com, 5 November 2018
11. 'Lufthansa, EasyJet among seven bidders for ailing Alitalia', rte.it, 17 October 2017
12. 'FS launches bid to acquire Alitalia', railjournal.com, 2 November 2018
13. 'Alitalia's two years in administrative limbo', flightglobal.com, 1 May 2019
14. Caswell, Mark, 'Easyjet withdraws from Alitalia takeover discussions', easyjet.com, 20 March 2019
15. 'Alitalia's two years in administrative limbo', flightglobal.com, 1 May 2019
16. 'Alitalia', eng.wikipedia.com
17. 'Alitalia's two years in administrative limbo', flightglobal.com, 1 May 2019
18. 'Atlantia to become Alitalia's majority stakeholder', airlinegeeks.com, 17 June 2019
19. Ibid.
20. 'Rome to take full control of Alitalia in June: minister', Reuters.com, 23 April 2020

Chapter 13
1. 'Efromovich, former majority shareholder of Avianca, and USAerospace seek to meet with Italian authorities to invest in Alitalia', gestion.pe, 22 May 2020
2. 'Michele Edwards of WOW 2.0 now displays a keen interest in Alitalia', simpleflying.com, 27 June 2020
3. 'USAerospace partners says still interested in Alitalia', Reuters.com, 22 May 2020
4. 'USAerospace, Efromocih interested in Italy's Alitalia', macaubusiness.com, 22 May 2020
5. 'German Efromovich et USAerospace prets à investor dans Alitalia', zonebourse.com, 22 May 2020
6. 'Efromovich, former majority shareholder of Avianca, and USAerospace seek to meet with Italian authorities to invest in Alitalia', gestion.pe, 22 May 2020
7. 'AeroItalia', eng.wikipedia.org
8. Berberi, Leonard, 'Alitalia lite un imprenditore il marchio storico', Corriere.it., 2 December 2021
9. 'Alitalia', eng.wikipedia.org
10. 'Alitalia relaunches with new execs, new name, new routes', Ch-aviation.com, 3 July 2020

11. Buyck, Cathy, 'Alitalia successor ITA Confirms October 15 launch', ainonline.com, 24 August 2021
12. Berberi, Leonard, 'Alitalia lite un imprenditore il marchio storico', Corriere.it., 2 December 2021

Chapter 14

1. Souza, Lukas, 'Italy's ITA Airways carries 9m passengers in its 1st year', simpleflying.com, 14 October 2022
2. 'ITA Airways', eng.wikipedia.org
3. Hendry, Jonathan E, 'ITA Airways records full year net loss despite Revenues Exceeding euro 1.5 billion', simpleflying.com, 29 March 2023
4. Ibid.
5. 'ITA Airways Board of Directors approved the preliminary Financial Report for the year 2022', ITA Airways press release, 29 March 2023
6. Landini, Francesca, 'ITA takes off, ending Alitalia's turbulent life' Reuters.com, 15 October 2021
7. Berberi, Leonard, 'Ita Airways, arriva la proposta di Indigo Partners', corriere.it., 11 March 2022
8. 'Delta, Air France-KLM eye majority stake in ITA Airways', Reuters.com, 10 March 2022
9. 'Lufthansa Group reaches agreement on the acquisition of 41 per cent stake in ITA Airways', Lufthansa Group press release, 25 May 2023
10. 'Eindelijk officieel: Lufthansa wordt aandeelhouder van ITA Airways', luchtvaartnieuws.nl, 25 May 2023'
11. European rules regarding state aid violated by Alitalia loans', moneyreview.gr, 27 March 2023

Appendix 1

1. 'Alitalia flight 112', en.wikipedia.org.
2. 'Italy jet crash kills 115", *The Lowell Sun*, 6 May 1972, https://web.archive.org/web/20111111012927/http://montagnalonga.wordpress.com/foreign-press/
3. Hradecky, Simon, 'Accident: Alitalia A321 en route on Apr 24th 2011, attempted hijack', www.avherald.com, 24 April 2011.

Other books you might like:

Airlines Series, Vol. 14

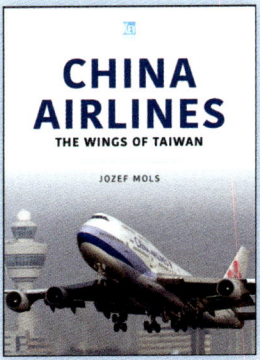
Airlines Series, Vol. 11

Airlines Series, Vol. 7

Airlines Series, Vol. 5

Airlines Series, Vol. 3

Airlines Series, Vol. 15

For our full range of titles please visit:
shop.keypublishing.com/books

VIP Book Club

Sign up today and receive
TWO FREE E-BOOKS

Be the first to find out about our forthcoming book releases and receive exclusive offers.

Register now at **keypublishing.com/vip-book-club**

Our VIP Book Club is a 100% spam-free zone, and we will never share your email with anyone else. You can read our full privacy policy at: privacy.keypublishing.com